THINKERS OF
OUR TIME

SCHELER

THINKERS OF OUR TIME

SCHELER

Francis Dunlop

The Claridge Press
London

First published in Great Britain 1991

by The Claridge Press
6 Linden Gardens
London W2 4ES

Printed by
Short Run Press
Exeter, Devon

ISBN 1-870626-71-0   (Hardback)
ISBN 1-870626-76-1   (Paperback)

Dunlop, Francis: *Scheler*

1.   Political Science
2.   Philosophy

CONTENTS

PREFACE

Max Scheler is one of the "great unknowns" of modern philosophy, yet at his death in 1928 Heidegger called him "the most powerful philosophical force in today's Germany, nay, in today's Europe — even in contemporary philosophy as such".

Apart from translations, this is the first book entirely devoted to Scheler to be published in the United Kingdom. It is aimed at all those who would like to know something of this remarkable thinker, and accordingly I have tried to make it as untechnical as I can. I have not done a lot to put Scheler in his historical context, or provided much in the way of criticism. Instead I have concentrated on giving the reader some idea of his central concerns and the way he tackles them. I have tried to bring out the interconnectedness of Scheler's thought, and the book is, therefore, best read in the order in which it is printed.

Norwich

2nd May 1991

REFERENCES AND TECHNICAL TERMS

Where books and articles by Scheler are referred to in the text their titles are translated into English. The first time I give the full title, afterwards I usually give an easily identifiable abbreviated one. Quotations from Scheler are also translated, but all detailed references are to volume and page numbers of the German Collected Edition (GW). Information about this and about translations can be found in the Bibliographical Notes at the end. All translations in the text are my own. The biographical information nearly all comes from *Scheler*, by Wilhelm Mader, to whom I am much indebted.

All German terms used by Scheler as technical terms are explained or translated somewhere in the text, usually at their first appearance. Use of the index will help the reader to track these down.

1. SCHELER'S LIFE AND INFLUENCE

Max Ferdinand Scheler was born in Munich on the 22nd August, 1874. The Schelers had long been pillars of bourgeois professional society in Coburg, Upper Franconia, from where his father administered the Hungarian estates of the King of Bavaria. His Jewish mother, Sophie Fürther, came from a respectable and orthodox family about whom little seems to be known. Shortly before Max's birth his parents moved to the Bavarian capital, a change which seems to have been the result of his mother's boredom with provincial life, and her desire to be near her wealthy unmarried brother, from whom a handsome inheritance might be expected. For the father it meant a complete upheaval, and brought on a slow decline.

The maternal uncle was also orthodox, and the young Max was brought up, very much against his inclinations, in a strict but outward observance of the Jewish faith. His mother spoiled him atrociously, and was correspondingly hard on his younger sister Hermine, who took her own life at the age of sixteen. Max did very badly at school, and had to be sent to a cramming establishment, where his precocious interest in Nietzsche was noted. About this time he seems to have become romantically attracted to Catholicism, towards whose richness of ceremony and symbol he was favourably disposed. He eventually qualified for university studies from the Ludwigsgymnasium.

As a reward for this his father treated him to a holiday in the South Tyrol, where he met Amélie von Dewitz-Krebs, the woman who was to ruin his early career and absorb much of his spiritual energy for many years. She was several years older than Scheler, married, and had a daughter. The attraction was mutual and irresistible, for Scheler the first of many.

In the summer of 1894 he began his university studies in Munich, and enrolled for philosophy and medicine. Next year he moved to Berlin, where Amélie lived, and then to Jena, so as to study under Rudolph Eucken, who is usually classified as a neo-Kantian. Scheler's preference for philosophy had been clear from the start, and medicine was neglected. Eucken especially drew him because of his emphasis on the spiritual and personal, and his unconventional activist conception of philosophy. In December 1897 he graduated with first class honours. In his philosophical dissertation *The Relations Between Logical and Ethical Principles* (GW I) he argues that there is no satisfactory way in which the search for knowledge can be harmonised with the moral demand.

A growing interest in sociology took him to study briefly under Max Weber in Heidelberg. But he returned once more to Eucken at Jena to qualify for university teaching. His thesis, *The Transcendental and Psychological Methods*, was accepted in 1899, and presents a critique of the two philosophical approaches prevalent in Germany at the time — the transcendental, harking back to Kant and largely concerned with the question "What makes knowledge possible?", and the psychological, which interprets knowledge reductively as the mere workings of the human brain according to natural scientific laws. Scheler's solution — the "noological" method, which accepts a distinction between spiritual and psychological phenomena — owes much to Eucken, but also shows his own growing independence (GW I).

The same year saw Scheler baptised a Catholic, married to Amélie, and starting his university teaching at Jena. Shortly afterwards he met Husserl, the founder of the phenomenological movement, with which Scheler became closely associated. In 1922 Scheler mentioned this meeting — the first of many — in an article entitled *Contemporary German Philosophy* (GW VII). He says that both he and Husserl expressed their independent conviction that far more could be intuited, or directly apprehended, than was acknowledged by the Kantians, who confined intuition to the contents of sense perception. Notwithstanding this avowal of an early interest in the phenomenological approach, with its concern to establish the essential contents of all kinds of experience, there are few traces of it in the three short pieces Scheler published after his thesis at Jena. He was still under the influence of neo-Kantianism.

In 1906 came the first of the scandals provoked by his wife. She publicly accused the wife of a well-known publisher of carrying on an affair with her husband. Scheler was forced to resign his post. With the help of Husserl he was able to transfer to Munich, where he began to lecture early the following year.

Scheler's interest in phenomenology must now have been greatly strengthened. Munich possessed an active circle of phenomenologists, whose leading lights were Johannes Daubert, Alexander Pfänder and Moritz Geiger. Scheler quickly achieved an influential position among them. Among his best-known pupils and closest friends was Dietrich von Hildebrand, son of a well-known sculptor. But, although much of his later phenomenological thought was worked out in his lectures and conversations, and his outstanding ability became widely acknowledged, Scheler published nothing during this period. Geiger later said that what above all attracted Scheler to phenomenology was its concentration on intuition and the discovery of essential connections between things. Scheler also brought to it what phenomenology had hitherto lacked: a "world-view" into which individual insights could be fitted. This was the religious "philosophy" of Catholicism.

It seems clear that at this time much of Scheler's energy was being dissipated in coping with his marital difficulties and other personal problems. An even more destructive scandal broke out, and dragged on until 1910. It now seems that the original case was based on an absurd misunderstanding. But Amélie and her mother encouraged the press to hound Scheler, and there were many people glad of an excuse to discredit the university. At first the professors rallied to Scheler's defence, but in 1910, when he was accused of having borrowed money from one of his students, they lost their patience. Scheler's licence to teach in German universities was withdrawn.

To begin with it seemed that he might take up a position in Japan or Egypt, whence offers had come. But nothing materialised, and he went to Göttingen, the most important centre of phenomenological studies at the time. The question of finance must have weighed heavily on him, since he had no private means. He was partly supported by von Hildebrand, who hired a hall in which Scheler could give unofficial lectures. These also had the blessing of the Göttingen philosophical society, among whose members were Husserl and the other phenomenologists Adolph Reinach and Theodor Conrad.

In 1912 Amélie at last consented to a divorce, leaving him free to marry Märit Fürtwängler, sister of the famous conductor, whom he had come to know and love when she was a student of his in Munich. But Amélie's price was the whole of the substantial legacy Märit was to inherit from her dead father when she came of age. Scheler and his new wife settled in Berlin.

There seems little doubt that the marriage to Märit gave Scheler the atmosphere he needed for productive work. But the couple had nothing to live on beyond what Scheler could earn as an unsalaried academic. He continued to lecture in Göttingen, and also in Berlin, where he took up journalistic activity for a time, but his days were largely spent in philosophical writing. The next few years saw a great flood of publications, including the first editions or first parts of "Resentment in the Structure of Moral Systems" (GW III), *The Essence and Forms of Sympathy* (GW VII) and *Formalism in Ethics and Non-formal Value-Ethics* (GW II). His importance in the world of learning was recognised in his coeditorship of Husserl's phenomenological year-book. Apart from his phenomenological works (articles on self-deception, virtue, the Tragic, in GW III, and on shame, GW X), Scheler also produced a substantial number of philosophical papers on social topics, such as feminism, insurance pensions and the bourgeois ethic (GW III).

When war broke out in 1914 Scheler fully shared the general mood of enthusiastic relief. He tried to enlist in the Air Force, but was rejected because of his astigmatism. At once he turned back to writing, and very quickly produced an article "The Spirit of War", which was expanded into the first of his "war books" in 1915. These writings on the first world war (GW IV) have always been a stumbling-block for liberal defenders of Scheler, since they seem to glorify war and are full of attacks on liberal principles. Staude has seen in them evidence that, in his social and political philosophy, Scheler was little better than a time-server, who followed the public mood like a weathercock. It is certainly true that Scheler was always responsive to the atmosphere that surrounded him, and that these books and articles won him fame throughout the German-speaking world. But his enthusiasm soon wore off, and the later books contain passages critical of Germany, in which he calls for moral and spiritual renewal. Besides, they are not mere propaganda, but seek to penetrate the universal meaning and value of events and institutions.

Scheler's religious commitment, already apparent in his immediately pre-war works, became stronger during the war, and he published several articles on social, political and religious themes in the Catholic periodical *Hochland* (GW IV and V). In a country where the religious-intellectual scene had been for so long dominated by Protestants, Scheler was quickly recognised as a major apologist for Catholicism. His growing fame, the inspirational quality of his lectures and speeches, and his anti-English and anti-American sentiments (chiefly inspired by his hostility to Utilitarianism), led to his being recommended to the imperial authorities for propaganda work among the Catholics of Switzerland, Austria and Holland. Scheler himself used these opportunities to go on developing his own never wholly orthodox thinking.

The end of the war saw the *de facto* lifting of the ban on Scheler's university work. Konrad Adenauer, then mayor of Cologne, saw in him the academic heavyweight he needed to represent the Catholic interest in the newly refounded university. In 1919 Scheler took up his position as University professor of philosophy and sociology, and head of the Institute of Social Sciences.

But he was never happy in Cologne, and tried almost from the beginning to move elsewhere. At first his publications reflected the hopes of Adenauer and those others who appointed him. There is a great deal on sociology and social questions (mostly in GW VI), and the beginnings of a sociology of knowledge and culture (GW VIII). But, after the publication of *On the Eternal in Man* (GW V) in 1921, the culmination of his Catholic-inspired religious philosophy, there were signs of unorthodoxy in religious fundamentals. Quite soon Scheler let it be known that he no longer considered himself even a theist "in the usual sense". This was a severe blow to a great many religious believers who had taken comfort from his writings, and controversy still continues over the causes and exact significance of this apostasy.

One theory is that Scheler's real enemy was the institutional church. Shortly after his arrival in Cologne he had once more fallen seriously in love with a much younger woman. Maria Scheu was very different from his second wife Märit, and much more able to enter into his philosophical speculations. Scheler tried to persuade Märit to accept a triangular relationship, but she refused. He then tried to persuade the Church authorities to let him divorce her. This was also refused. Scheler's turn from a personal creator God is supposed by some to be the result of this rejection. Others simply pointed to the steady evolution of Scheler's thought.

It is clear that Scheler must have been under severe emotional strain during this time. He had a heart-attack in 1920, and at the beginning of the following year Amélie got the guardianship of their son Wolfgang, who had grown up a psychopath, transferred to him. Friends from this period speak of incessant chain-smoking and heavy drinking, and his need to forget himself in company — any company where he could find an audience, however unsuitable, for his unquenchable flow of ideas. In 1923, however, Märit consented to a divorce, and he married Maria the following year.

Scheler's philosophy in the middle '20s shows a great increase in speculation, going with an increasing interest in the sciences. There is a gradual shift of focus from social-philosophical questions to metaphysics and philosophical anthropology. Some saw in this Scheler's "Break-through to Reality", a much-needed supplement to his studies of essence and essential relations. Others derided it as the proof of intellectual breakdown. Most Catholics felt let down, but some of his greatest contemporaries, including Heidegger and Hartmann, were much impressed. Whatever the truth of the matter,

Scheler entered a real physical decline during these years. His new marriage also brought new problems, and his letters testify to a deep unhappiness and isolation. He made increasingly desperate attempts to move elsewhere, and received many offers to lecture abroad. But, despite his popularity as a lecturer and conference speaker, a role in which he could still hold the most diverse audiences spellbound, his efforts to escape from Cologne were frustrated. Only in 1928 did he receive a long hoped-for call to Frankfurt.

His relief was short-lived. A few days after his removal there, while Maria was still in Cologne and bearing his child, he had another heart-attack and died a few days later on May 19th. He was buried in the South cemetery in Cologne, as a son of the Church. The child he had always longed for, a son, Max Georg, was born on the 28th December. Many moving tributes were published in the press and in philosophical journals, acknowledging Scheler's greatness and lamenting that the work to which he had dedicated his last years was still unfinished.

In 1929 Maria Scheler set to work to produce a collected edition of his writings. Scheler had left behind enormous quantities of material, and it was hoped that his philosophical anthropology, metaphysics and philosophy of history, sketches for which were contained in lectures published during his life-time (GW IX), might also be included. But, although a volume of early papers was published (GW X), work on the *Nachlass* proved exceptionally difficult. Then, in 1933, the Nazis forbade the publication of anything by Scheler, because of his maternal Jewish descent. However, Maria continued her work, and gradually, from 1954, the volumes of the collected edition began to appear. On her death Max Georg Scheler entrusted the editorship to Manfred Frings, but his residence and teaching in the USA, together with the still chaotic state of much of the remains and the need to reissue the published works, meant that only in 1979 was a volume of material relating to the last period of Scheler's life published. This volume, containing sketches and fragments on metaphysics, has since been joined by another on philosophical anthropology (GW XI and XII).

As I have already intimated, Scheler was extremely well-known in

Germany and other parts of Europe between the wars. His books were widely discussed, his lectures were packed, and his audience stretched far beyond the confines of the university. But he never came near to founding a "school", as Husserl did. It is easy to see why. Quite apart from the unorthodox nature of his career, Scheler never really brought anything to a conclusion. Even his best writings look forward to other works, which will properly establish important insights, or provide essential additions to the topic discussed. There is no real consolidation in his thought, but rather a series of brilliant and profound insights, with some extremely promising preliminary analyses. Scheler is always "moving on" somewhere new, both as a thinker and as a man. His work does not lack coherence, despite surface inconsistency, but this is because it all expresses the man. Just as Scheler himself never really grew up, so there is little that seems "established" enough, either in theme or in method, for any community of scholars to extend and adjust.

This does not mean that he was totally without influence after his death. It is rather that his influence has always been "inspirational", scattered and personal, rather than institutional. A thoroughgoing "Schelerian" is not easy to imagine. But many thinkers have been greatly stimulated and provoked by his writings, especially in ethics, philosophy of religion and philosophical anthropology. Among philosophers we may mention Nicolai Hartmann and Dietrich von Hildebrand, whose ethical works owe much to Scheler. Cassirer, Maritain and Berdyaev were also influenced by him. His ethics helped to pave the way to Existentialism (Marcel, Sartre and even Heidegger are indebted to him), and the enthusiasm of Ortega y Gasset resulted in the spread of phenomenology, including Scheler's own work, to Spain and thence to Latin America, where his influence has perhaps been more lasting than anywhere else. One must not forget that Scheler has also been as influential, if not more so, in the social and human sciences. Arnold Gehlen owed a great deal to Scheler, as did Karl Mannheim, Karl Jaspers and Philipp Lersch.

What about the present? The last war, with the Nazi proscription of his work, the discomfort felt by many liberals at the earlier "war books" and the vitalist streak in his thought, which seemed uncomfortably close to Nazi thinking, seems to have created an effective barrier between Scheler and the modern student of philosophy, especially in the USA. Recent philosophical fashions, above all in the United Kingdom, have in any case put him firmly beyond the pale. Post-war translations have done something to extend people's interest, but some of these have been scarcely adequate to win Scheler many new friends. But if *The Philosophers' Index* is any indication, there is a steady minority interest in him, especially in Germany, Latin America and parts of Eastern Europe (Pope John Paul II wrote a thesis based on Scheler). Nevertheless, far too many publications still assume virtual ignorance of his work, and there is little sustained discussion of his thinking,and scant development of Schelerian projects. One can only hope that this situation will change.

2. ETHICAL PERSONALISM

Scheler's most substantial contribution to ethics is his book *Formalism in Ethics and Non-formal Value-Ethics*. This classic of "applied phenomenology" is of central importance for the understanding of Scheler's work as a whole. Despite its enormous length (nearly 600 closely printed pages of text), the work was never conceived as a complete ethical treatise, but as a clearing of the ground for one. The title obviously refers to Kant, whose formalist ethics, despite many attempts to refute it, was still enormously influential in Scheler's Germany. Scheler himself admired Kant's work, but associated it with the neglect of love and joy that he saw in the Prussian ethos. So he felt that the essential thing was to provide a general refutation of ethical formalism, with (somewhat erratic) reference to Kant. As a result, only a small proportion of the work is devoted to ethics as it is usually understood today, and what there is is full of tantalising gaps. A great deal of the book is taken up with a critique of Kant's moral psychological presuppositions. The many subtle analyses of experience this gives rise to were to prepare the way for his own "ethical personalism", as he calls his own position. The main principle of this is that "the ultimate sense and value of the entire universe is ... to be measured by the pure being (not the achievements) and the most perfect possible goodness ... of persons" (GW II 16). I shall try to bring out the personalist emphasis in a survey of the main ethical features of the work.

Let us return to the "non-formal ethics" of the work's title. Most ethical theorists have tried to derive moral principles from some determinate good or purpose, such as happiness or self-fulfilment. Kant assumed that these and any other non-formal and determinate principles could only be derived from contingent experience. As such they would be products of Man's "sensibility", and could not have the objectivity and universality which a rational ethics required. There must then be a formal moral principle not derived from experience but "prior" to it (*a priori*); for Kant this meant that it must be the product of the reason with which we order the contents of sense experience. Kant's *a priori* moral principle is thus a universal "law" which the rational subject gives to himself.

Scheler accepted that Kant had definitively disposed of any ethics of goods or purposes. These must be relative to changing historical situations or subjective preferences. But he argues, applying the phenomenological method to moral experience, that an absolute and objective system of material values is "given" to everyone as the foundation of moral and practical choice. There are in fact at least four modalities of value quite distinct from one another and forming a hierarchy. The hedonic values of the Pleasant and Unpleasant form the lowest kind. Above them come the vital values and disvalues, such as the values of health and strength, or efficient vital functioning, and their negative counterparts. Scheler also follows Nietzsche in including in this category the values of nobility and baseness, in the sense of good or bad 'stock' or 'breeding'. Above them again is the tripartite sphere of spiritual values, containing aesthetic values, the values of justice and injustice (which underly the idea of just law) and the values of "pure knowledge of truth". At the summit of the hierarchy come the values of Holiness and Unholiness. In the second part of *Formalism*, written a little later than the first, the values of Utility and their opposites are inserted as a fifth category immediately below the vital values. The rank ordering of the value modalities also forms part of the material data of ethics. It seems to be implied in Scheler's system that there are also rank-orderings between particular values, but he does not say anything about them.

Scheler called values "the emotional *a priori*". They are emotional because they are intuited or apprehended in feeling. They are *a priori* not because they are *produced* by feeling or any other faculty, in Kantian fashion, but because they are fundamental and irreducible data. Goods are goods because they have value, goals and purposes are only intelligible when something is striven for as having value. Even pleasure is always sought because of its value. Values are, then, material qualities of things. That they are not mere logical or linguistic abstractions from their "bearers" is shown by experience. We may, for example, meet a person for the first time and be aware of some exceptional spiritual quality about him without knowing what. Or we sense the high aesthetic value of a work of art before we have really taken in its sensory elements. Or we feel "the atmosphere of a value" in memory, perception or anticipation, before its bearer is given to us at all. In the same sort of way we may find ourselves half-consciously "striving for" something we feel to be very important, without having clearly conceived what it is, or accepted it as one of our goals. In such cases we are guided by an awareness of value that precedes our knowledge of what exactly it is we are after. In Scheler's view, our feeling-apprehension of the world precedes our intellectual grasp. The world is first given as valuable in various ways; only subsequently do we see it neutrally, as though it were "value-free".

The hierarchy of material values is not the only fundamental ethical datum. There are also hierarchical orderings of "relatively formal" values, depending on the essential natures of value-bearers. Thus there are rank-orderings between the values attaching to persons and those to things, between values attaching to the person, possessions, acts, etc. of another and those of oneself, between the values of acts, functions and reactions, between "*Gesinnung*-values, action-values and result-values", values of one's intention and one's state. Within personal relationships Scheler distinguishes and orders the values of the persons involved, the form of their relationship and the actual relationship as they experience it. There are the orderings between the values of the individual *qua* individual, and *qua* representative of some group he belongs to. Finally (and this category is very important) there are relations between "values in their own right" (the basic material values) and values given to us as having derived validity (as with tools).

Lastly, Scheler takes over from Brentano four extremely formal principles of value — namely that the *existence* (or realisation) of a positive value is itself a positive value, that of a negative value a negative one, and analogously with the inexistence of negative and positive values respectively.

Scheler's ethics is, then, based on the claim that we have access to an ordered realm of values of various kinds, which, to put it in terms more familiar to English readers, provide all the different sorts of objective "reasons" we may have for our value-judgements or practical decisions, and grades them for us. The "ideal" realm of values is not derived from contingent experience, like the particular goods and purposes we may be moved to pursue, but is "prior" to it, in that it is in its light that goods and purposes appear as such. Certainly we have to have experience of things to feel values, since they are always "borne" by *something* (though it could be something imagined or fictitious). But one "taste" of, say, dishonesty is enough to tell us at once that it is a negative value (of justice).

We have also seen that values are given in feeling. Scheler also says that they are the "correlates" of feeling. This is an instantiation of one of the most important principles of phenomenology — the correlation between types of spiritual act and types of "object" — to which we shall return more than once below. It is of importance to us here because of what it tells us about Scheler's doctrine of the person.

Both Kant and Scheler maintain a duality in the human being, and connect human worth or dignity with the superior of the two aspects. Scheler calls this the "person", and contrasts it with the ego, or *Ich* (I), the subject of the psycho-physical organism. The distinction between the aspects can be partially resolved into one between spiritual acts and vital "functions". My ego is "functioning" when seeing, hearing, feeling or, activity is simply "going on" in me, whereas I am fully gathered "in person" in every one of my acts, and actively "perform" it, so that questions of meaning and validity necessarily arise. Thus the person can be said to act *through* his ego and (some of) its functions, a manner of speaking which is appropriate both to actions in the full sense and also to more passive and receptive acts of intellectual or emotional intuition. But Kant, at least in Scheler's view, saw the person wholly in terms of rational operations (leading to either judgment or will). Against this Scheler insists that a wholly intellectual being would not be a person, and that a person is essentially a source of acts of all possible kinds, including acts of love and value-feeling, which have nothing to do with intellect or will at all. If anything takes the place of Kantian Reason in Scheler's philosophy it is *Geist* (Spirit). Persons, In Scheler's view, are the places where Spirit appears. Acts of all different kinds are spiritual. But Spirit is essentially individualised, not universal and general like Kant's Reason.

The person, then, is a "unity of being" of spiritual acts, and gives spiritual meaning and value to the vital functioning of an individual human animal. The realm of material values can then be regarded as the correlate of all possible spiritual acts of feeling, or as the "world" in its axiological aspect. This is the reason why this realm does not contain *moral* values. For moral values are the values of persons. Just as persons are not "parts" of the world, because they are the correlates of the world, each individual person being correlate of his own "microcosm", so moral values cannot be parts of the "axiological world". And just as persons cannot be known as objects, even to themselves, since the world is the sum of all possible objects, and they are not parts of it, so the pursuit of one's own moral value is self-defeating, and becomes the Pharisaical pursuit of self-interest.

Scheler found it difficult to conceptualise his insight into the nature of the person. He says that persons are not objective substances. Their "being" is completely in every one of their acts, and changes morally with its performance. However, they do "found" their own acts, and must therefore be *something* apart from their acts. The most Scheler will allow is that they are "act-substances". If, and only if, they wish to reveal themselves, they can be known through "co-performance", "pre-performance" or "after-performance" of their acts, as we think their thoughts after them, and so on. This seems to be possible because spiritual acts must inform vital functioning, which *is* part of the world. This knowledge of persons requires sympathy, and sympathy is only possible because all human beings share in the same life which pulses through all living things. But there is an "intimate sphere" at the heart of every person which is wholly unknowable.

We have already seen that values, for Scheler, are given in feeling. This is not the feeling of feeling-states, such as anxiety or elation, but a *sui generis* act (based on a function) in which something is apprehended. It enables us to grasp first the mere presence and then, as we concentrate, the full material quality of values. But the comparative height of values is given in another kind of acts, which Scheler calls *Vorziehen* (preference) and *Nachsetzen* (putting after). These are also intuitive acts of feeling, and likewise have nothing to do with willing or choosing, or any other kind of act, and cannot be further analysed. Scheler does actually mention certain "criteria" of value-height. Higher values have more essential durability than others (love is given as "for ever"), they are less in need of division to be shared (compare a work of art with a loaf of bread), less dependant on other values, more deeply satisfying and less relative to feelings whose presence depends on vital constitution (see below). However, these criteria have no logical role in actually establishing precedence, but are derived from experience. They will, at best, assist or prompt us to feel it.

But he sometimes says that the value-realm is the correlate of love, and talks of the *Ordo Amoris*, using the term both to indicate the ideal ordering of loving for each individual or social person (see next chapter), and also the ordering that actually obtains. Love is in fact a central concept in Scheler's philosophy, and Man is often defined as the *Ens Amans*, the being that loves. Scheler sees himself here as the heir of Plato, Augustine and Pascal, and pours especial scorn on those thinkers of the Enlightenment who reduced love to sympathy or altruism. He says that it is love, in modes ranging from vital interest to spiritual love, that makes possible all other kinds of mental or spiritual directedness to things, since these all entail that the individual goes out of himself into the world, or "transcends" himself. But spiritual love, which founds value-preference, is not itself any kind of feeling according to Scheler — it is perfectly compatible with violent changes of feeling about its object - nor is it any kind of judgment, wishing or willing. Its object is always an object *qua* value-bearer. But it is not directed to this object simply as it empirically is, but as it "is-

and-might-be", or as it "ideally" is. Thus Scheler insists that love is a "movement", from given values to possible higher ones (hate goes in the opposite direction). It grasps its object "in its *terminus ad quem*". But love doesn't necessarily try to produce these values in any way. There is absolutely no pedagogical or "bettering" intention in love as such, nor anything conditional on the appearance of higher values. It is simply that the object of love is the entire object, as it is and as it might be, and the lover (of the object) "moves" from the realised value which first occasions love to the higher unrealised values in the "value-picture" he dimly senses as foreshadowed in the values already realised. It is this movement that makes love "creative". Thus the lover sees far more in the beloved than other people. If he is merely infatuated, his "love" will be blind. But if he truly loves, he will enable new and higher values to shine out in the beloved.

This analysis of love comports well with the idea of a person as an axiological direction or tendency (see below). But the analysis of the "substance" of love largely takes the form of a *via negativa*. Scheler is so concerned to say what love is not, and to insist on its uniqueness, that he omits to say what "genus" of spiritual act it belongs to. Elsewhere there are indications that he sees it as more like willing than intellectual intuition or value-feeling. He also calls it a "movement of the heart" in *Sympathy*, and says that it presupposes an impulse towards the same value-sphere intended by the act of love. It also involves "a warm, emotional and unreserved affirmation of the reality and *Sosein* of the object". Whatever the truth of the matter, it is love for things, especially persons, that founds value-preference, by bringing new (and higher) values to light. "Preference" thus has something to work on, and the act reveals the relative height of the values feelingly grasped. Acts of pure value-feeling, in which our grasp is made more precise and exact, are then founded in their turn in acts of preference. Scheler's emphasis on love is thus a central aspect of his Ethical Personalism.

In Kant's view, love could only be morally significant if it were "practical", that is, willed in the form of an act of kindness or something similar. The will is the locus of the moral value of the individual. Scheler, on the other hand, finds this locus in the *Gesin-nung*. One might translate this as "disposition", did this word not sound too anaemic and even superficial to capture Scheler's meaning, which corresponds roughly with the old idea of the "heart", the deepest aspect of spiritual-psychic life, and the source of all good willing, pure intuition and right loving. As against Kant's "will", the *Gesinnung* gives a much stronger suggestion of moral *being*, of the moral quality of acts as expressing the person, rather than the moral quality of the person being dependant on his acts.

These ideas are further extended in Scheler's theory of *Vorbilder*, or personal models. Since it is love that opens up the world of values for both individuals and societies, and the highest love is the love of persons, persons play an enormous part both in moral education and in historical change, for which change of social ethos, under the influence of élites and *Vorbilder*, is in Scheler's eyes fundamental. A *Vorbild* does not have to be an actually existing person, since fictional, legendary and mythical ones can also be personal models. But they must be the personal embodiments of values, and be such that individuals will be drawn to them out of love so that they will themselves be transformed after the pattern of the *Vorbild*. The "imitation" concerned is the more effective the more unconscious it is. But it does not connote manipulation on the *Vorbild*'s part — he may be quite unconscious of what is going on — since the person imitating feels his transformation as a realisation of his true nature and an expansion of his being. *Vorbilder* do not in fact choose people to influence (Scheler had an extremely low opinion of the effectiveness of all moral pedagogy); rather, they are themselves chosen by their followers, who sense in the values presented by the *Vorbild* a pattern for their own self-realisation. Nor do *Vorbilder* do away with individuality, since the person "imitating" is realized — becomes himself — in the process of imitation, and persons are necessarily individual.

Scheler's theory of *Vorbilder* is incomplete. He planned a long work on the subject, of which we have only fragments. But it is clear that he regarded it as an essential part of his "material", or personal, ethics. He also stresses that there is a hierarchy of ideal *Vorbilder* corresponding to the hierarchy of values, so that we have the saint at the top, then the artist, the lawgiver and the sage, then the hero and the "leading spirit of civilisation" (inventor, entrepreneur, and others concerned with "utility" values), and lastly the "artist of enjoyment". Scheler's often rather sketchy descriptions of these types are full of interest.

We have already alluded to Scheler's theory of individual value essences. It provides one of the ways in which he emphatically defends objectivism in ethics while equally emphatically rejecting universalism. As we shall see in the next chapter, there are social persons as well as individual persons, and the theory applies to them also. These ideal essences are as objective as any value or general essence. Love for *Vorbilder* plays a vital part in their realisation. To any individual concerned, realising oneself is like creating a work of art. One has initially a shadowy inkling of one's value-essence, and this receives greater and greater definition in the actual process of realisation, but the "rules" one "follows" are largely unconscious. The realisation of one's individual essence constitutes one's "personal salvation", and the spiritual feelings (see below) of blessedness and despair are the index of whether one is or is not on the way to achieving it and how far one has to go. The knowledge of a person's essence is also accessible to other people, if their understanding of the person is based on love. This goes also for the person whose essence is in question, so that self-love is necessary if a person is to discover his own personal salvation. But, if another loves him better than he loves himself, he may have the right way pointed out to him by this other. Personal existence is, then, essentially a direction.

A closely related idea is that some values are only given to individuals, both personal and social. Indeed, such individual values are the highest there are. Both individuals and moral communities must therefore apply themselves to the cultivation both of what is a value for all, and also of what is a value for them alone. Only so can one hope to have complete insight into what is good-in-itself. Scheler argues that an insistence on general validity, in values as in norms, can only betoken moral decline and subjectivity. At the social level the "*Forderung der Stunde*" (demand of the hour) must be quickly heeded or it will pass away for ever unrealised. It is not to be thought of as the application of general principles to a unique historical situation, but as the "call" of historical "situation-values".

The individual's moral task (and salvation) in life is, then, to bring his actual loving into line with the objective good for him. Some of the content of this will be good for anyone, some only for him. If he does that, then the right conduct will follow as a matter of course, since, given a knowledge of one's situation, adequate feeling-cognition of value, founded in correct feeling-preference and love, will immediately determine the will. The morally good act is thus the act whose intention is the realisation of the value given as higher (or highest) at the time.

But this picture appears to leave no place for one of the most fundamental moral data — the experience of obligation. Scheler's general position is that obligation is founded on the experience of values but only appears when value-apprehension is defective. Unlike his followers in material-value ethics, Hartmann and von Hildebrand, he denies that value is ever equivalent to an "ideal obligation", or general "Ought-to-be", on the ground that all "oughts" are addressed to particular persons. Nor, he says, can a value be interpreted as a kind of transcendental pressure or demand (such as "the voice of God"). For value is a kind of self-subsistent quality (though attaching to objects), quite "indifferent" to the realisation of its content. However, he makes an exception of Brentano's formal principles of value (see above), and says that it is these principles-about-principles which provide the bridge between material values and general ideal obligation.

Scheler also tries to discredit obligation altogether. He says that an Ought-to-be can only become an Ought-to-do addressed to a specific individual if the latter apprehends it as addressed to his condition, one of reluctance to act in conformity with the principle. Thus the same general value-principle, for example that all persons should be treated as of equal value, may result either in an individual's treating himself better than others, or the reverse, depending on whether his usual inclination is to favour himself or others. And in general, says Scheler, the emphasis on obligations goes with an atmosphere of negativity and restraint, it implies an inadequate grasp of value, a lack of moral maturity and a realisation of moral evil. Appeals to obligation and duty are all too often strategies to dispense with moral thinking, or with taking full responsibility for our acts. Despite these observations, Scheler does recognise the validity of general moral principles and their obligatoriness as a kind of minimal morality, provided they are derived from some individual *Vorbild* or "social person" experienced as exemplary. Even submission to authority and tradition may bring the individual into some contact with positive value, and help him to see for himself. But Scheler cannot for long withdraw himself from the Utopian vision of the free spirit who chooses the good naturally as soon as he sees what it is.

Later in this book we shall be looking at Scheler's philosophy of religion. But we must note that there is a surprising amount of talk about God, as *summum bonum* and supreme "person", in *Formalism*. Both Scheler's ethics and his idea of the person seem to require the existence of an absolute being. He claims, for example, that all lower values are founded on higher. This seems to mean that the values of pleasure and pain would lose their "validity" (their real status as values) if there were no health and vitality in the creatures whose sensations were in question. Vital flourishing would seem in turn to lack real significance (it would be mere "birth, copulation and death") if there were no superstructure of spiritual values. Again, these values would themselves be nothing *sub specie aeternitatis* without the supreme values of holiness and unholiness. But if there were no supreme being in whom these values were realised, all lower values might seem to lack validity. In connection with the person, the being of God seems necessary to make sense of personal value-essences and the individual-person-relative values connected to it. The former are ideas in the mind of God, the latter have their objective place in the whole realm of values as the correlate of God's love, just as the personal "objects" and "microcosms" of individual knowers are

unified in the "Macrocosm", which is the correlate of God's knowledge.

Yet Scheler was happy to approve the third edition of *Formalism* in
1926, after he had officially renounced theism, and denied that the
work presupposed either the essence or the existence of the Christian
God. Indeed, he says here, far from being grounded on the metaphysics of absolute being, it is ethics which supplies evidence for the latter.
It is, therefore, as features of experience that we should test Scheler's
ideas about value, not as items in a logically watertight theory. It is
also worth reminding ourselves that the pre-Christian Plato also put
love at the centre of his philosophy and regarded persons very highly,
being "adopted" by many of the Church Fathers as a believer before
his time. Religious language can also be given metaphysical and
psychological as well as confessional interpretations.

3. THE SOCIAL WORLD

Scheler's philosophy of persons-in-society is at first presented as a natural extension of his ethics, but serves increasingly as a foundation for his pioneering sociology of knowledge and culture. Apart from these more theoretical studies, his many publications on social issues show a burning interest in the current social questions of his day. These are integrally connected with his philosophical ideas on the social being of Man, which we shall concentrate on here.

In his *Problems of a Sociology of Knowledge* (GW VIII), Scheler opens the section on formal problems with a brief exposition of the "most fundamental axioms of the sociology of knowledge" (55ff). Here he claims that the *Mitwelt*, or social and historical world of "the other", is one of five irreducible spheres of being given to every human consciousness from the beginning of its existence. With whatever detailed content these spheres are actually filled, it must be in the following order: the Absolute, the *Mitwelt*, the inner and outer worlds together with one's own body and its environment, living beings and, finally, non-living things. Furthermore the earlier spheres are always fundamentally more real to us than the later ones, and thus the last to be authentically doubted or explained away. There have never been any real solipsists, says Scheler, though the later spheres of reality have all been seriously questioned.

Characteristically Scheler leaves the "strict proofs" of this thesis for a work that was never written. However, the arguments he gives in *Sympathy*, which he also gestures towards here, suggest that he was relying at least in part on the evidence of anthropology, child development and abnormal psychology. We shall return to his discussion of the Absolute below. As for the *Mitwelt*, he claims that we can still occasionally experience the whole world as a vast "field of expression", with which "social" relationships are possible, in a

way more characteristic of young children and primitives (see next
chapter). This means that at first we only perceive things to the extent
that we can grasp them as unities of outward expression and inner
state, like a smiling face. This field becomes gradually differentiated,
as friendly or hostile concentrations of egocentrically significant
expression begin to stand out with the help of social interaction, and
we become aware of the definite distinctness of certain individuals
(making no distinction between real people and other "animate"
objects). At first we relate to ourselves as to others, as the people
around us do, and only later do we feel a special affinity with the ego
socially indicated as peculiarly our own. This social derivation of the
idea of Self makes self-knowledge much harder than it is usually
reckoned to be, and most of us still have difficulty in distinguishing
what we really want, feel and believe from what other people do. But
increasing sophistication enables us to fill out the essential spheres of
outer and inner worlds, and of our own "lived bodies" and their
environment, as we become gradually aware that there is both an inner
and an outer side (which may not keep in step with each other) to the
frowns, smiles, embraces or clenched fists that constitute perceptible
expression, and that our ability to control "body" in general is
confined within the limits of what we now experience as *our* bodies.
Finally, the sphere of "living thing" is filled out by contrast with the
things in which no changing expression, and therefore no possibility
of relationship, can be made out: the sphere of "dead" nature. The
development of individuals and of cultures thus involves a process of
increasing "disillusion", as the appropriate field for earlier affective
forms of relating is reduced in scope and gives place to more prosaic
but effective ones.

In *Problems* this thesis is used as an argument to show the socially
conditioned nature of all knowledge. Because "We" is given before
"I", our first knowledge takes the form of what "we" (all) know. But
the thesis is also related to Scheler's solution of what English-
speaking philosophers call the Other Minds problem. We have
already touched on Scheler's theory of our knowledge of other
persons. In *Sympathy* (GW VII 209ff) Scheler discusses two contem-

porary theories of what he called knowledge of other egos. One of these is the argument from analogy: I notice that some of my own feelings, say, are regularly accompanied by certain outwardly observable movements of my body. I also observe similar movements in similar bodies around me. I therefore conclude that similar feelings occur in these bodies also — in other words, that there are people like me, of whom I can have some knowledge.

Scheler points out that both this and the argument from "empathic projection" presuppose that our knowledge of other egos starts from (a) a perception of their bodies as mere physical objects and (b) an assumption that all subjective experience is our own. Both these presuppositions are false. Besides appealing to the developmental sequence we have set out above, Scheler argues that the situations in which we *do* find ourselves arguing "from analogy" are always abnormal ones. We know, for example, that some intention is being expressed, but are puzzled as to its exact nature. Children also have knowledge of other minds, but they first manifest it long before they can make inferences. One cannot live with animals without some awareness of their changing mental states. Animals clearly also show some awareness of the mental life both of their own and other species, including ours. Some of this may beg the question, but it is certainly part of our naive experience of things. And in any case, says Scheler, the analogical argument would really only entitle me to conclude that my own ego was also in the other body; it would be going too far to conclude to the existence of another ego.

Scheler also has another argument for the primary givenness of the *Mitwelt*. He pictures a Robinson Crusoe, alone on his desert island, with absolutely no knowledge of human society. Such a man, says Scheler, would nevertheless become aware that somewhere there must be a community of similar beings to which he belongs. For there is a class of acts which essentially require the existence and response of others to be meaningful. Examples are command, obedience, promising, gratitude and love. Our Robinson Crusoe would find himself feeling the impulse to perform such social acts, but in a meaningless, or "unfulfilled", fashion. This absence of fulfilment would itself reveal to him the (here empty) sphere of the *Mitwelt*. This argument of Scheler's is another application of the general phenomenological principle that act and object are in essential correlation. It assumes that acts are not just opportunistic reactions to contingent experience, but are directions already "built in" to human life in which correlative objects are actively sought. It has much plausibility if we conceive of our nature's having evolved to fit its environment. There are passages in which Scheler hints at such an argument, but seems for the most part simply to assume it.

I turn now to Scheler's theory of the forms of social relatedness. In *Formalism* he sketches out four different essential types of social unity or relatedness — that of mass- or herd-life, that of *Lebensgemeinschaft* (life-community), that of association (*Gesellschaft*) and that of *Gesamtperson* (corporate person), or *Liebesgemeinschaft* (love-community), the moral community of totally personal relationships. In the "mass" the relationship is at a very low level of human functioning indeed, since there is no mutual understanding between individuals, or any experience of individuality, and the "relatedness" is constituted by psychic "infection" and involuntary imitation. Scheler later added "identification" as a special case of this type of unity. We shall expound Scheler's understanding of these matters below.

The second kind of social unity — life-community — is most conspicuous in close family life, primitive tribes or traditional peasant communities. Here there is mutual understanding of its members in a common mind. Awareness of oneself as an individual is not primary, but results from "singularising acts", in which one artificially separates oneself from the whole. The basic sense of responsibility is thus corporate, with individual responsibility founded on it. Individuals are "replaceable" by others of the same caste, status, dignity, office or calling in respect of some aspect of community life. But there is nothing personal about the life-community. Its life is governed by custom and ritual, which are expressions of its pre-conscious and quasi-automatic striving and value-preference.

The third form of social unity is *Gesellschaft* (association). This kind of relating can be seen most clearly in the company set up to achieve some limited purpose. It is thus essentially artificial, and all relationships are deliberately initiated as between individual "self" and "others". Understanding of others is here built on inference, and any "common mind" depends on conscious agreement. Responsibility is primarily individual, and any responsibility for others must be based on specific commitments. Nor is there solidarity, but merely equality or inequality of the interests of individuals, or the "classes" they constitute. Unlike life-community, association has no reality independent of its members, since it is a network of obligatory relations. Whereas the basic attitude of the former is trust, that of the latter is mistrust. On the other hand association, unlike mass and life-community, is a manifestation of *personal* life, albeit in a form restricted to individual persons, who relate to each other merely as formal equals. Not surprisingly, association is only possible for adults.

The fourth variety of social unity is "the unity of autonomous and spiritual individual persons ‘in’ an autonomous and spiritual individual community". Scheler usually calls this the *Gesamtperson* (corporate or total person). Here there is both full individual and irreplaceable personal being and community membership, and also consciousness of them, there is responsibility for self both on the part of the individual and of the community, and also shared responsibility of the individual for the community and of the community for each of its members. This shared responsibility relates not only to the individual's place in the community as a structure of relationships but also to his possession of a unique and individual conscience, since the "Good-in-itself for me" must affect the "Good-in-itself for all". This points to the universal solidarity of all moral beings, since, whatever social acts we perform, it lies in the essence of the understanding of these acts to make some personal response (even a refusal to respond), and the whole moral universe must therefore necessarily be affected in some degree. There is, therefore, no sphere of moral privacy.

In his sociology of knowledge, Scheler approaches these distinctions by describing the ways in which an individual can share in the experiences of his fellows. We find here identification, unreflective identity of experience through "infection" and blind imitation of actions and expressive movements, also direct understanding, and then again inference, which correspond to Scheler's first three types of social unity. But, in place of something clearly corresponding to the *Gesamtperson*, we find the claim that shared experience founds two categories indispensable to the sociology of knowledge, the "group psyche" (or ego) and the "group spirit". We are not to understand these as "metaphysical entities, which really precede shared life and shared experience, but simply as the subjects of the psychic or spiritual content continually recreated in this sharing" (GW VIII 54). The group psyche, functioning unreflexively and quasi-automatically, produces myth, folk-tales, ordinary language, folk-song, folk-religion, custom, and so on, whereas the group spirit, in full awareness and deliberation, creates the state, law, the language of culture, philosophy, art, science and public opinion. The group psyche is impersonal, whereas the group spirit depends for its ethos and direction on personal leaders and models, on an élite. But these products of the group psyche and spirit die out unless individuals reperform the acts necessary to keep them alive in an essentially participatory fashion. That is, both folk- and high culture and their institutions have to be nurtured by our continual reaffirmation of them, not as entertaining historical survivals, but as "ours". We do this not as individuals but as group-members.

But we must return to the forms of social relating. In reality none of them is ever found existing by itself. Historical social unities display them all, and receive their distinctive individuality through their particular mix of these elements, and the concrete forms through which they are realised. But these ideal essences represent a necessary framework within which all historical development has to take place. Nor do they form a straightforward hierarchy. Certainly mass-life comes at the bottom, and purely personal community comes at the top. But the other two forms are axiologically on a level, and are equally necessary to *Liebesgemeinschaft*, the one contributing the necessary solidarity, and the other the realisation of individual personhood.

Scheler's analysis is confused by the fact that the term *Gesamtper-son* seems to denote both an essential form of social unity, *Liebesge-meinschaft*, and also any really existing social group. In this sense he conceives of the *Gesamtperson* as a social person. It is constituted by the social acts and shared experience of individuals, but transcends any particular individual. Like an individual person, it has its own correlative "world" (*Gesamtwelt*), which sets limits to the micro-cosms of its members, and is the bearer of moral or personal values, with its own "personal" vocation and axiological "direction". The moral code of a society, or smaller community, has the kind of moral authority over its members possessed by *Vorbilder*. The situation of the *Gesamtperson* is also structurally analogous to that of the indi-vidual. As the body-soul unity is to the person, so are the actual life-communities, associations and masses to the *Gesamtperson*. It fol-lows that not all human social relationships can be purely spiritual or personal. Society needs the kind of unreflective, customary, even "primitive" forms of behaviour so often derided by enlightened liberals, as we individually depend on efficient psychic and bodily functioning. A nation which, for instance, encouraged associational, or contractual, forms of relating, at the expense of the vital together-ness of traditional family and community life, would eventually disintegrate because, among other things, the ability to make con-tracts and agreements and stick by them — which is the fundamental way in which co-operation can be achieved in *Gesellschaft* — depends not on some general contract to keep contracts but on the fraternal and solidary sense of obligation felt by the members of a life-community to realise the values they experience as binding for it. All *Gesellschaft* is both essentially and in practice dependent on *Gemeinschaft*.

Scheler's social criticism and social-philosophical outlook are closely bound up with the general ideas set out above. In keeping with his Personalism, his most general concern is the extent to which social conditions and institutions make possible the flourishing of persons. Any promotion of policies which might seem to *replace* rather than supplement the personal acts of love-community with institutional "caring" would arouse his deepest misgivings. But his outlook finds perhaps its most concentrated form in his attack on the bourgeoisie and the spirit of Capitalism. Scheler devoted three essays to this subject, but several of his other writings, especially "Resentment" (GW III), are relevant. Scheler here argues that Nietzsche was wrong to accuse Christianity of resentment. It is the modern humanitarian ethos which is born of ignoble weakness and consequent denial of vital values. Christian love is fully appreciative of these. Its renunciations are based on the vision of values inestimably higher, which Nietzsche failed to see. It should be added here that Scheler soon came to see the good side of humanitarian love, though continued to hold that it was especially liable to be an object of resentment from those who could not rise to the axiologically higher forms of Christian neighbour love and love of one's country.

As regards the bourgeois ethos, Scheler sees it as epitomising the modern attitude to the world. It is not only to be found in Capitalism but also in the class-consciousness of the proletariat and in much State socialism. Its fundamental mark is a distortion of human value-experience. In particular it neglects the claim of vital values, and exaggerates the importance of hedonic and utility values. This is manifested firstly in a fanatical concern with work and making money, which leads to a subordination of ends to means and a desire to dominate reality rather than enjoy its values and qualities. The Bourgeois becomes a utilitarian ascetic. His self-centred distortion of value takes two forms, according as he feels stronger or weaker. He either becomes a careerist or is consumed with bitterness. In the first case he measures all value in relation to his striving for what is bigger and better; in the second he denies the value he sees around him because it is not his.

Scheler particularly associates the bourgeois with egalitarianism. This is completely hostile to the values associated with "being", especially vital values, and tends to deny any value that is not worked for and attainable by all. The bourgeois ethos is also antipathetic to moral solidarity, where the main concern is the fact that values have been realised, not the identity of the realiser. The emphasis on

individuality leads to an undue stress on *Gesellschaft* and the consequent growth of mistrust, and the cult of the divisive hedonic values.
The bourgeois mentality, Scheler thought, also leads inexorably to
value-relativism, and to the confusion of values with desires. The
institutionalisation of these things is especially furthered by the
morally and spiritually feeble, who cannot bear to acknowledge their
own inadequacy. As compensation there is a disproportionate stress
on control of the world, and all forms of knowledge tend to become
'technologised'.

Scheler was of course perfectly well aware of Man's need for
technology. But he argued that it did not so much denote an extension
of his vitality as a substitute for it. The desire to control the world was
also in itself a natural expression of man's unquenchable desire for
happiness. It became harmful when it led people to ignore, or, worse,
take a reductive attitude to, the Spiritual. He accepted that the real
meaning of civilisation was the possibility of freeing the person from
menial tasks. All that can be done by machines *ought* to be so done,
he wrote. Metaphysically speaking, work was the imparting of
meaning and value to what previously lacked it. Nevertheless, all this
became the curse of humanity if it destroyed contemplation, admira-
tion and enjoyment of the inexhaustible richness and beauty of the
world, and the grandeur of fully developed personal and spiritual
being.

4. FEELING AND SYMPATHY

Scheler's work on feeling, emotion and sympathy is often regarded as among his best. It does, in fact, pervade everything he wrote, and we give examples of it elsewhere. In this chapter we shall concentrate on two things, his theory of the stratification of the emotional life, and his treatment of sympathy. Both of these accounts are quite detailed, and will give the reader some idea of the kind of close analysis Scheler was capable of.

The stratification of the emotional life receives its most extensive discussion in *Formalism* (GW II 331-45). The context is his criticism of Kant's claim that any material value ethic must make happiness, and indeed pleasure, the supreme criterion of ethical value. Scheler thus introduces his stratification to establish a new solution to the problem of the relation between happiness and morality.

He first points out that groups of related terms like bliss, happiness, cheerfulness, serenity, comfortableness, pleasure, and the like, on the one hand, and despair, misery, unhappiness, sadness, grief, unpleas-antness, and so on, on the other, are sometimes taken to denote degrees of intensity in, or differences in the accompanying sensations or objective correlates of, qualitatively undifferentiated emotional states. But in fact they refer to groups of positive and negative feelings which are quite different in themselves. Strictly speaking, one cannot feel bliss in relation to events which might also afford one pleasure. Sadness and the pain of, say, toothache are completely different qualities of feeling. But two or more feelings of these kinds can coexist in the same person; a blissful man can be in pain — indeed the martyr's bearing of his pain may itself be blissful. A deeply unhappy person may feel pleasure at a glass of wine. In such cases positive and negative feelings are actually present at the same time. They do not come and go as attention switches from one to another, nor do they merge into a unified feeling-state. Even the expression of such "contrary" feelings betrays elements of both, as a serene countenance remains serene despite the sadness expressed in its weeping.

All this shows that *depth* is an essential characteristic of both feeling-functions (and the emotional acts founded on them) and also feeling-states. This depth of feeling shows four major gradations. "There are 1. *sensory feelings* ...., 2. *feelings of the lived body* (as states) and *life-feelings* (as functions), 3. *purely psychic feelings* (pure ego-feelings), 4. *spiritual feelings* (feelings of the person)" (GW II 334). It will be clear that these gradations reflect the fourfold hierarchy of material value-types. Both of them reflect the hierarchical structure of human being.

The shallowest kind of feeling is sensory feeling. Pain and pleasure, in their various varieties, are always states, never functions. They have no relation to the "person", and only a doubly indirect relation to the ego, via the fact that they occur in "my" body, and then again in a particular "part" of it, which can change. They only exist as actually occurrent, and cannot themselves be reproduced, or felt "after" or "with" someone. Unlike all the other kinds of feeling, they have no essential relations of affinity or repugnance with any other feeling, but just "happen" and then, usually very quickly, pass away. Their "essential duration" is thus the shortest of any feeling-kind. They are not affected by being attended to (if anything, they increase with it). Of all feelings these are the most easily brought under our control (by the application of relevant techniques or drugs). It follows from this last fact that "practical Eudaimonism", in which states of emotional satisfaction are identified as the goal of moral and political action, tends to become fixated on sensory pleasure, and to encourage Hedonism.

The second level of feeling comprises, firstly, "feelings of the lived body". This kind of "life-feeling" in its various modes (well- and ill-being, freshness and exhaustion, health and sickness) pervades the body without being specifically localized "in" it. It is thus related to the ego at only one remove. Whereas in psychic feeling I myself, as ego, am glad, in life-feeling it is rather that I feel "myself" to be comfortable, the "myself" here denoting the "body-self", which forms a kind of back-cloth for the appearance of spatially isolated organ-sensations and organic feelings. Secondly, the lived body feeling is a single and relatively steady feeling in relation to sensory feelings, which can come and go without affecting it. Again, whereas sensory feelings are "dead states", with, at most, an objectively established "symptomatic" function, all life-feelings are in themselves "intentional", since in them we directly feel "life itself" in us, as it ebbs and flows, and also the vital values of our environment, as in the freshness of the forest, or the surging power of new Spring greenery. Of even greater importance is the role life-feeling plays in sympathy and knowledge of others' feelings, and hence the consciousness of community (*Gemeinschaft*). This means that we can also participate in our own past life-feelings. These feelings are subject to disturbance when attended to, and are less easily controllable than sensory feelings, usually requiring a complete change of vital regime, and within limits set by inherited dispositions.

The "functionality" of life-feeling comes out preeminently in a second group of feelings, including dread, foreboding, disgust, shame, relish, distaste, vital sympathy and antipathy, and vertigo. Scheler does not clearly indicate how far what he has already said about lived body feelings also applies to this sub-group, and there are other uncertainties in his account. But in contrast to sensory feelings, they indicate the value of what is to come, rather than that of what is present. Hence they are a kind of "distance-feelings", both spatial and temporal (as against sensory feelings, which are "contact-feelings"), and directly, but sub-intellectually, indicate the vital value of events and processes both within and outside our bodies, so that we may be pre-rationally prompted, as it were by the body itself, to take avoiding or exploiting action.

Psychic (*seelische*) feelings, such as joy, sorrow, gladness, nostalgia, form the second deepest category. These are unmediated feelings of the Ego, intentionally directed to perceived, imagined or fantasised objects. There is no spatial extension whatever in, say, grief. Although psychic feelings can vary in respect of the ego's involvement, and can be variously coloured by differences in life-feelings, the stratification difference between them and life-feelings is very marked. We might gloss this by pointing to the "open" and "rational" character of psychic as against vital feelings. Psychic feelings, Scheler goes on, can also be re-felt as "the same", and, because of their essential dependence on the world "outside" the Ego (though including the "self" as object of representation), are only in a very restricted sense under the control of the will. They do, however, tend to dissolve when closely attended to.

Spiritual feelings, such as true bliss or despair, serenity, peace of mind and the pain of conscience, are never states. They stream forth from the intimate depths of the person (in Scheler's technical and completely unlocalised sense) and transform what is given in spiritual acts with an all-encompassing light or darkness. They have thus an absoluteness about them, and it makes no strict sense to say we feel blissful or despairing *about* something. Other feelings can temporarily displace them, but, once they are given, they pervade the whole of our existence. We do not really *feel* bliss or despair. Rather we *are* blissful or despairing, as "we find an emotional Yes (or No) at the heart of our personal existence and our world", which is the index of our relation to our own value-essence. But, just as we necessarily cannot pursue moral value, so these "spiritual feelings" are the furthest removed from the control of our will.

Scheler's account of emotional stratification is not without its obscurities and apparent contradictions. It suffers from being an incidental, probably "dashed off", account in a work full of equally original and equally unconsolidated insights. Its main point is to show that Kant's ethical postulate of a divine retribution after death, which is supposed to satisfy once and for all the impersonal requirement that the good deserve to be happy and the bad unhappy, makes no sense, since moral goodness and badness have their *source* in spiritual feelings, which really characterise the person, and cannot possibly be "requited". But the stratification theory as a whole is important, both for what it does to make us sensitive to the richness and variety of feeling and emotion, and in what it indicates about the structure of human existence.

I turn now to a survey of some of the main features of Scheler's work on sympathy. I shall be basing my account on the first part of the second and much expanded edition of *Sympathy* (1922) (GW VII), which shows him moving towards his later metaphysical thinking.

He begins in chapter I with a general attack on a sympathy-based ethics, arguing that sympathy, though possessing moral value in its central form, is in itself blind to qualitative value (one may sympathise with a moral monster), and that a *spectator*'s judgements (the reference is to Adam Smith's ethics) cannot *make* acts good or bad, or show them to be so; they could in fact easily lead a guilty person to feel innocent, and the reverse. He cites the fact that many women accused of witchcraft came to share the general "spectator's" view of their culpability.

He goes on in chapter II to distinguish *Mitgefühl*, the most general German equivalent of "sympathy", from "*Nachfühlen*", which is often confused with it. The latter means feeling the *quality* of another's feeling "after" him. He asks us to imagine a child screaming itself blue in the face. A person may feel the quality of the child's feeling — it is perhaps lost — without actually suffering himself, let alone suffering *with* the child, as sympathy would require. This cognitive ability to feel the quality of feelings "after" their subjects without necessarily sympathising with them is invaluable for historians or novelists, and is analogous to "seeing" a landscape or "hearing" a tune in one's head. The upshot of all this is that sympathy, either as "co-suffering" or as "co-rejoicing", presupposes knowledge of another's pain or joy, but is quite distinct from it. As we have already seen, this knowledge of other minds is, for Scheler, founded on the "universal grammar" of expression.

Having based sympathy on *Nachfühlen*, Scheler distinguishes four different phenomena which are or could be called kinds of *Mitgefühl*. First there is the direct sympathetic feeling of, say, one and the same pain "with someone". Scheler calls this *Miteinanderfühlen*. "Father and mother stand by the dead body of a beloved child. They feel with one another 'the same' pain, 'the same' grief. It is not that A feels this pain and B feels it too, and they both also know that they feel it — no, it is a *feeling with one another*" (GW VII 23). Scheler points out that this could not be the case with sensory feeling. Here there would have to be fellow-feeling "with" another's feeling, as in the next type.

In the second type B suffers, and this suffering is an object for A's sym-pathy, or co-suffering. The suffering and the sympathy are experienced as two quite different things, since the first is a state and the second a function. B's suffering must first be given to A in *Nachfühlen*, and his own *Mitfühlen* is experienced by him as a "reaction" to this "material". The fact that the reaction could be one of pleasure at B's pain shows the distinction clearly. The sadist is thus not in the least "insensitive" to the pain of others. Insensitivity is shown when the person concerned is so sunk in his own feeling that he cannot make himself cognitively receptive to that of another. All this has its analogues in joy and "co-rejoicing".

In the third place comes *Gefühlsansteckung*, literally "feeling-infection" — not really a true case of sympathy, says Scheler, but often confused with it (e.g. by Nietzsche, whose "devaluation" of sympathy is based on this confusion). An example is the case where people newly arrived at a party are at once "infected" by the jolly atmosphere, even though they may have been feeling sad, and are "drawn in" to it. They do not "intend" the merriment of the others, as in *Mitgefühl*, nor do they participate in the same feelings. They may leave the party, and find themselves still feeling elated some time later, and have to *think about* what caused them to be in that state. Even real feeling is not necessary for this "infection", since it can be induced by the "objective feeling qualities" of dull weather, or a serene landscape. This shows that "infection" is not essentially bound up with imitation, as is sometimes held. It is also characteristic of "feeling-infection" to intensify, as the individuals concerned re-infect each other. Thus they can find themselves behaving in ways they would not have dreamt of on their own. The process underlies many of the phenomena of "fashion", "public opinion", and genuine "tradition". It is characteristic of all these that the judgements and evaluations they give rise to are erroneously considered by their authors as their own, and as objectively founded.

The fourth phenomenon — *Einsfühlung*, "feeling one with" — is really a limiting case of the third. Here there is unconscious and unwilled identification of one or more egos. Scheler at first presents two ideal types of this. In the "idiopathic", B's ego completely absorbs A's, so that B no longer experiences it as having rights of its own. In the "heteropathic" type B is so "hypnotically rivetted" by A that he "lives entirely in", or "through", A. Scheler finds actual cases of these in totemism, where, for example, the members of a tribe identify themselves with red parrots. He also suggests that ancestor-cults, which presuppose separate identity, denote a liberation from an earlier stage of complete identification, and likewise that the wide-spread belief in reincarnation is but a rationalisation of *Einsfühlung*. He sees full cases of heteropathic *Einsfühlung* in the mystery cults of the ancient world. Here, he says, we have identification in *Dasein*, since the initiate's object is to identify with the actions and life-history of the God; in cases of lasting hypnosis, on the other hand, the subject, all unaware of what is happening, feels at one with the hypnotiser in his *Gesinnung*, and we have a case of *Sosein*-identification. Again, he sees the masochist, who frequently exchanges roles with his sadistic partner, as driven not by a simple desire to be dominated, but by "an *einsfühlende* interest in the dominance of his partner, that is, a *sympathetic acquisition of power*" (GW VII 33).

Scheler also describes cases of *Einsfühlung* where individual iden-tities are "fused", for example in a loving sexual act, where the personal centre is ecstatically inactivated and both partners seek to be immersed in a "single stream of life". The orgies of the Bacchic mystery cult relate to this. This kind of identification also occurs between the members of a crowd or "mass", whom a Führer has absorbed into himself. The "single stream of feeling and impulse" sweeps all participants along with it like leaves before a storm. We also find this type in the instinctive bond between a mother and her baby. It *can* develop into an idiopathic variety ("smother-love"), but, in the normal case, the pre-puerperal "vital and psychic unity" remains after the birth, so that the mother "knows" the condition of the child from her own vital-psychic experience of oneness with it. Scheler also sees this "feeling-identification with the one life-process, which flows from a single centre", in other creatures. It underlies, for example, the instinctive "understanding", possessed by certain species of wasps, of the anatomy and life-processes of certain caterpillars and other prey. They sting them in exactly the right place, with just enough venom to lame and not kill, so that they may lay their eggs on them. He suggests that this "foreknowledge" through *Einsfühlung* of the specific dynamic structure of the alien life-drive has its parallel in human perception, which is at first of significant fact-value structures pre-given in imagination, and merely indicated by the various senses, and not of factual and valuational elements subsequently combined. This is an element of Gestalt psychology.

All the examples of *Einsfühlung* so far exemplified come from childhood, exceptional life-states, pathology, primitive society or the life of animals. Yet Scheler holds that it underlies all genuine understanding of living things. We are in fact in danger of losing the faculty, as increasing emphasis is put on higher mental functioning. But the human race would be the poorer for this, and hence arises the ideal of exploiting the contribution of all peoples, both sexes, all conditions of humanity, if we are ever to achieve a truly comprehensive grasp of things.

Scheler locates *Einsfühlung* in a sphere of "vital consciousness" which lies between the personal-spiritual level and the level of the "lived body", with its own feelings and sensations. In both the latter we are given to ourselves as individual, whereas the correlate of "vital consciousness", "the objective organic life process", is something general. It is noteworthy that all varieties of *Einsfühlung* take place "automatically", as the result of "vital causality", which is distinct from both rational motivation and mechanical causality, and is characterised by "automatism, directedness, *vis a tergo* and determination by the individual's past as a whole". It can also only take place when our spiritual and bodily spheres are relatively "empty" of contents. One must raise oneself "heroically" above individual bodily concerns and let drive-directed life "flow on" by itself, but also become "smaller" than the person of reason and dignity by "forget-ting" one's spiritual individuality. Thus all treatment of people as a "crowd" or "mass", as in war or revolution, makes both heroes and idiots of them.

In the third chapter Scheler refutes various genetic theories of sympathy in the light of his analyses. The idea that all sympathy contains an element of "reflection", amounting to the question "what would it be like if that happened to me?", rests on the Enlightenment prejudice of the essentially egotistical nature of Man. Such an idea confuses real sympathy with cases like that of the man whose "sympathy" rests on his need to be surrounded with smiling faces, or to be left undisturbed by others' pain. They also fail to distinguish between feeling-states and feeling as psychic function. If A really sympathises with B he feels (this is the function) B's feeling-state, and the latter does not transfer itself to A, or produce the same state in him. Even in one's own case the feeling of pain and the pain felt are distinct, and not essentially coordinated. Scheler also describes a series of cases in which people live at second-hand, wholly from the pictures that others have of them, or "for effect". Although such cases have been interpreted in terms of intensified sympathy, even "sacrificial" behaviour, they lack the experienced "distance" from others and the sense of self-worth which are an essential precondition both of true self-sacrifice and of sympathy.

Scheler also considers another type of genetic theory, in which the perception of the movements that express another's joy or pain is supposed to bring about, either directly or via a tendency to imitation, a reproduction of similar feelings previously experienced in oneself. Scheler answers that true sympathy betokens true self-transcendence. The kind of theory in question merely explains certain frequently occurring factors that stand in the way of sympathy, or distort it, as when the "comforter" in whom one confides one's sorrow cannot stop telling us about similar painful experiences of his own. The theory also makes the unjustified assumption that one must oneself have suffered something, or "something like it" (but how like it exactly?, Scheler pertinently asks), in order to sympathise with the sufferer.

Only in the case of sensory feelings (especially "perverse" ones), which, we recall, have no real meaning in themselves, is it difficult to sympathise without relevant experience. But many even of the life-feelings of animals (exhaustion, fear of death) are perfectly intelligible, let alone the higher feelings of human beings. The theories in question overlook the widening of experience which sympathy can bring, dismiss as illusory the "moral solidarity of mankind", and deprive sympathy of all its moral power.

In chapter IV Scheler discusses metaphysical theories of sympathy, arguing that in the ordinary practical attitude to things the being of other people is only given to us in a "shadowy" form. Only in true sympathy is the illusory nature of this "Egocentrism", in which "my" world and "the" world are one and the same, and the existence and value of the other is relative to the "absolute" value of oneself, revealed. For in *Mitgefühl* we grasp a truth which might be expressed in these words: "The other is of equal value to you, both as human and as living being; he exists as truly and as genuinely as you." (This, of course, does not mean that all people's "contingent natures" are of equal worth.) Sympathy, then, is an *a priori* act in which the *a priori* content "*Fremdwert überhaupt*" (the value of other people as such) is given.

In his discussion of Schopenhauer's and E. von Hartmann's attempts to argue from the nature of sympathy to the essential identity of all persons, Scheler argues that it shows the exact opposite. Not only does it do away with the Egocentric illusion, but also disposes us to see "that independently existing persons in relation to one another are also by nature *'predisposed' for a communal form of life* and teleologically ordained for one another" (GW VII 76), since in sympathy we grasp "the harmonious value-complementarity" of persons. This essential "being-determined-for-one-another" demands an exalted "Reason" that determines. Thus pure sympathy, "just because it cannot be explained genetically through association", provides another argument for a single creator of the persons who all primordially share this feeling. True sympathy, then, in contrast to *Einsfühlung* and feeling-infection leads not to a pantheist-monist, but to a *theist* and possibly "panentheist" metaphysic. It also contains an insight into the essential transintelligibility of other persons, both in respect of their "intimate sphere", and also of the qualitative "otherness" of others' feelings, which we cannot fully penetrate. This is one result of the reactive nature of sympathy. It is not a "spontaneous act", and therefore has not the same power as love to get beyond that in the other person which is given to *Nachfühlen* in the everyday *forms* of interpersonal relationship.

Scheler sums up his remarks on the metaphysical importance of *Einsfühlung* thus: he inclines to the opinion that it is "a subjective indication of the metaphysical unity of everything living, an awareness of the same (where *Einsfühlung* is reciprocal), and finally the foundation in being for the real possibility of this phenomenon" (GW VII 85).

In his subsequent discussion (chapter V) of historical manifestations of sympathy, Scheler pays special attention to Indian philosophy (including Yoga techniques of self-mastery), the Greeks, and the hostility of Western Christian thought until the time of St Francis of Assisi, who is remarkable in Scheler's eyes for having combined *Einsfühlung* with all creation and spiritual identification with the person of Jesus Christ. The most striking feature of St Francis's attitude to Nature was its lack of any human reference. For him all natural phenomena had their own "expressive meaning". They all pointed directly to the creator, and did not require to be "interpreted" by us as so doing. They also constituted a "living whole", whose individual features could be compared to the different successive expressions on a single face. Finally, they all had their own relation to God, so could truly be called our "brothers and sisters". Scheler traces this discovery back to the originally Arab movement of courtly love in Provence. It is, in short, Eros which provides the foundation of *Einsfühlung*, and which has left many traces in St. Francis's own life and works. The saint in fact provides the most perfect example of Eros combined with Agape known to us. We shall see how Scheler developed some of these ideas in the chapter on metaphysics.

Chapter VI contains a brief discussion of the "foundational laws of sympathy". The first law is that *Einsfühlung* founds *Nachfühlen* (both taken in the functional sense). That is, in order to be able to feel X's feeling-states after him, I must have experienced the *qualities* of these states through *Einsfühlung* with his kind, whether this be living thing as such, human beings, people or family. We have already looked at Scheler's well-founded claim that *Nachfühlen* founds *Mitgefühl*. The third law is that *Mitgefühl* (or *Miteinanderfühlen*) founds humanitarian love, since only through it do we come to fill out the pre-given sphere of the *Mitwelt* (see above) with beings of "equal reality", which spontaneous love of "Man as Man" presupposes. *Nachfühlen* is insufficient, since its objects can be the states of fictional people. Finally humanitarian love founds Christian love of one's "neighbour" (i.e. the person one encounters anywhere) "in God". The reason for this is that the "persons" of all others without exception can only be loved if they are already given, and loved "up to the borders of personal being", as "equally real" members of the human species, rather than as "friend as against foe", "free man as against slave". Thus the Christian ideal could not gain currency in history until the way had been prepared for it by the late Hebraic and Roman ideal of "universal humanity".

We shall end this survey with Scheler's very brief account of the moral value of true sympathy, which constitutes chapter X. True sympathy is, in the first place, quite independent of any helpful *action* it may give rise to. Its intrinsic value is indicated by its nature as self-transcending on the one hand, and in the saying "a trouble shared is a trouble halved" on the other. As to the degree of moral value it exemplifies, this depends on (a) whether the feeling is spiritual, psychic, vital or sensory, (b) whether it is a case of *Mitgefühl*, or the axiologically higher *Miteinanderfühlen*, (c) whether it is directed to the actual feeling (as function) of the person suffering, or merely to his state, (d) whether it is directed to a higher or lower "state of values". If the person's suffering or rejoicing is truly proportional to its object, then *Mitfühlen* is of greater moral worth than if it is not. It is also greater if it is directed to the state of a more valuable person, less if to that of a less valuable one. This sketch may recall the tables of value-height in our chapter on Scheler's Ethical Personalism.

5. PHILOSOPHY OF RELIGION

Scheler's main contribution to the philosophy of religion is contained in *On the Eternal in Man* (GW V). This book was written during the first two years of his time in Cologne, and was widely discussed in Germany until the Nazi proscription of Scheler's work in 1933. It reveals Scheler's close, first-hand, contact with the phenomena of religion. This is very clear in the essay "Repentance and rebirth", with which the volume opens. Scheler here analyses repentance as a form of self-healing of the soul, through which it is in our power to alter the meaning and value of past events. He considered it one of his best works.

As we have already pointed out, his appointment to the Cologne Chair had a religious-political dimension. However, Scheler could not wholeheartedly subscribe to the official Catholic philosophy of Thomism. Nor, on the other hand, could he accept the Subjectivism of Modernist Protestant thought, in the Kant-Schleiermacher line. So one of his first tasks was to define his position in relation to these two dominant tendencies of thinking. He sees himself as providing a firmer philosophical foundation for religion by recourse to "the kernel of Augustinianism, freed from its historically conditioned husk, and to the methods of phenomenology" (GW V 8).

The main issue was the place of Reason in knowledge of God. Thomists believed that a great deal of the content of Christian Theism could be demonstrated to reason alone, and refused to draw a hard and fast line between theology and metaphysics. The Modernists tended to separate the two disciplines (if they accepted metaphysics at all) and to argue that God was not given to reason, but to subjective feeling. Scheler's solution is a kind of *via media*, and is based on a penetrating examination of religious experience, which enables him to make some important distinctions. His general position in *On the*

Eternal is that a complete knowledge of God requires both the rational
metaphysical and the non-rational experiential approaches, that the
metaphysical contribution is of very limited scope and that the non-
rational approach, which is essential for Christian thought, also yields
certainty.

For Scheler the only certain conclusion of metaphysical thinking
about the Absolute is that a first cause exists. This is the second of
what he calls the three foundational insights of philosophy. They are
put forward in the essay entitled "On the essence of philosophy and
the moral conditions of philosophical knowledge", contained in the
first part of *On the Eternal*. He pointedly compares his three
foundational principles, necessarily given in a certain order, with the
Cartesian starting-point. Descartes began with the certainty that he
was himself thinking (*cogito*), which puts the problem of knowledge
firmly in the forefront of attention. Scheler sees himself as reviving
the older "philosophies of Being", and argues that the first principle
of philosophy must be "that something exists, or, better, that 'there is
not Nothing'" (GW V 93). One is tempted to see in it the distinction
between order and chaos, or the intelligible and the unintelligible,
though there is nothing in Scheler's difficult discussion to suggest
this. Instead, he focuses on the affective contents that inform the
appreciation and neglect of this difference. The realisation that there
is something but might have been nothing is associated by him with
wonder and humility, as though all being were a gift one had no right
to expect.

This affective content appears again in his exposition of the second
fundamental philosophical certainty, which is that all Being (or non-
non-being, as Scheler prefers to call it) is either dependent on some
other being for its own being, or exists absolutely (by, through or for
itself). Whatever the exact nature of this dependence, or the mode of
the being in question, we see, says Scheler, that all dependent being
possesses a measure of non-being, which is attributable to these
dependencies. But the being it also possesses must have its source in
some being not subject to this limitation. This is not a variant of the
Thomist "first cause" argument, since it is not an argument, in the

usual sense, at all. Rather, Scheler is trying to show us that one may *see* the Absolute shining "through" the relative non-being of any dependent being. But, once more, we shall not see this unless we feel and wonder at the difference between the two types of being, dwelling especially on our own dependence, or non-absoluteness, and the gulf that separates it from absolute being, and humbly seeking to prevent our vision being clouded by the illusion that everything we have to do with, especially ourselves, exists "as a matter of course".

The third fundamental philosophical certainty, that every possible being has both essence and existence, need not detain us here.

Rational metaphysical knowledge of God comprises no more than this, that there is an absolute being which is the first cause of all other beings. There is for Scheler nothing here which could establish the nature of God as holy or as the *summum bonum* (highest good), let alone as personal.

All further knowledge of God depends on the performance of religious acts, which we are to see as a distinct class of acts. Religious acts include acts of repentance, petitionary prayer, thanks, praise, awe, reverence and worship. They are as fundamental to human consciousness as thinking, judging, perceiving and recalling, and must arise in any spiritual being conscious of its own mortality. They cannot be interpreted in terms of wishes or natural needs, or any combination of non-religious acts, because their objects belong to an essentially different sphere from the objects of other types of act. The three most important criteria of religious acts are their world-transcending intention, the fact that only the Infinite, or the Divine, can possibly fulfil them and the fact that they essentially look for an "answer" on the part of their object. The Divine to which they are necessarily addressed is given in the act as absolute and as holy, which, for Scheler, denotes the *Summum bonum*.

The absoluteness of the object of religious acts can, as we have seen, be at least partially given to the rational mind. But the meaning of holiness can only be understood in the performance of the acts. This also makes possible the attribution to God "by analogy" of human characteristics such as spirit, reason, will and love, though one is not deducing or inferring these qualities, but merely giving linguistic definition to qualities directly grasped through the act itself. On the basis of the experience which comes from performing the acts, one may even pursue something like the rational Scholastic science of analogy, and explore the essence of the Godhead as it is revealed, or symbolised, through the essential structure of the world. Thus the categories of number, time, space and magnitude yield, *per analogiam*, the divine qualities of absolute uniqueness, eternity, ubiquity and immeasurability.

The religious act also reveals God's nature as personal, and the fact that all religious knowledge of God is based on revelation. We have already noted Scheler's claim that persons have an "intimate sphere", to which they can withdraw without revealing themselves. All knowledge of persons thus depends on the consent of the person concerned. But we human beings cannot disguise our existence, since we are embodied. God, however, is not embodied and can not only freely refuse to reveal his nature, or essence, but even conceal his very existence — though his nature as all-loving, which we grasp in the religious experience of being loved, in fact prevents this. Thus all our knowledge of God is a knowledge through God.

Scheler argued that the sphere of the Absolute, and thus the tendency to perform religious acts, was given to all human beings. In *Problems* (GW VIII 56) he says that the sphere of the Absolute is even more fundamental than the sphere of the *Mitwelt*. It is therefore the first to be filled with definite content in all human development, and the reality of its contents is the last to be doubted or left undecided. Scheler seems to be saying that the child's (and indeed humanity's) first and most deeply embedded experience is of perfect objects and absolute qualities. Characteristically, he does not defend this claim (though it had been held by the 17th century thinker Malebranche), but it may help to recall here the kind of vision of infant experience typically presented by certain visionary poets, such as Traherne and Wordsworth, the aura of perfection that surrounds so many ordinary memories of early childhood, and the cultural universality of Golden Age myths. Scheler is, of course, well aware that many people do not believe in God, as "defined" by institutionalised religion. His claim is that every person must relate to *something* as to an Absolute, and that the dangers of self-deception are never so great as in the highest reaches of spiritual activity. The question for every person is, then, not "Do I believe in God?" (understood in terms of a particular creed), but "Is the object of my religious acts a really adequate one?" A "smashing of the idols" (money, fame, family, etc.), together with self-assertion of the spiritual person *vis à vis* the vital soul, is an essential preliminary to religious renewal.

The fact that everyone has a disposition to perform acts of this kind is, for Scheler, the nearest thing we have to a proof of God's existence (though see also the "proof" through sympathy outlined above). But he holds that the idea of proving existence is really absurd where anything other than the ideal "constructed" objects of mathematics are concerned. The traditional proofs were once regarded as indications of ways in which God can be directly encountered. Thus it is not so much the fact that human beings perform religious acts that counts in the end, as that God will reveal himself to one who performs the religious act in the proper frame of mind. It is only two monstrous prejudices — that all directly given objects are given to the senses, and that all undemonstrable things are hypothetical — that prevent more people, including many believers, from accepting this. We can in fact have complete certainty about God's existence in performing religious acts.

The metaphysical and the religious are thus two distinct roads to the apprehension of God. But the religious road, always based on revelation, is itself twofold, comprising both "natural" and "positive" branches. The natural way is independent of history, and can start from any finite object or event. The positive way is historically conditioned, since it depends on the existence of saints or *homines religiosi*. He sees an essential connection between the idea of God, the historical or sociological form of religious faith, and the personal transmission of revelation. He thus pours scorn on all impersonal theories of religious progress. The saint is the personal *Vorbild* in its most consummate form. Full religious knowledge is thus anchored in a *Seinsverhältnis* (relation of being) between the *Homo religiosus* and the community of faith. The individual must believe *as* a member of the "total person" of the Church, and thus make up for his personal limitations. Scheler's exploration of the institutions of Catholicism within this philosophical framework is full of interest and profundity, though he tended later to use these ideas to repudiate exclusive adherence to one religion, on the grounds that no one *homo religiosus*, and living tradition of discipleship deriving from him, could possibly possess the whole truth about God.

Scheler called his theory of the relation between metaphysics and religion a "system of conformity". While metaphysics starts from wonder and is concerned to grasp the nature of ultimate reality, religion derives from the desire for salvation, and aims at contact with the highest good. Hence its God is a "living" God, anthropomorphically described as wrathful, loving and forgiving, and encountered in practical life, whereas the God of metaphysics is conceived of as timeless and unchanging, the object of theoretical contemplation. Despite these and other differences, there is an ultimate coincidence in the objects of the two activities, based partly on the unity of the human spirit, which would not tolerate an ultimate duality, and partly on the *de facto* identity between the intentional objects of the two. For it must be the case that the salvation of all things depends on the nature of ultimate reality, and that the absolutely holy must be the absolutely real. Apart from that, the two approaches are needed as counterbalances to each other. The combined picture they yield, full of tensions though it may be, is nevertheless truer than either picture on its own.

6. FORMS OF KNOWLEDGE

In opposition to the tendencies of his day, Scheler saw his philosophy as a philosophy of being, rather than knowledge. Thus, instead of making an investigation into "the criteria of knowledge" the centre of his epistemology, he takes knowledge for granted, and focusses on the various ways in which its objects are themselves relative, and on the adequacy with which they are known. The most important question is always: *what exactly* is known?

The prime sources for his theory of knowledge are the posthumously published essays "Phenomenology and Theory of Knowledge" and "Theory of the three kinds of Facts" (GW X), a section of *On the Eternal* (GW V), "Idealism and Realism" (GW IX) and the collection of essays and lectures he gave in the last few years of his life, entitled *Philosophical World-view* (GW IX).

What, then, is knowledge? Scheler says that it is primarily a *relationship of being*, one of *participation*, in which one being, the subject, stands to another being, the object, without in any way changing it. Although the knower has to seek knowledge actively, he is completely receptive in the cognitive relationship itself. One implication of this definition is that not everything can be known. We should recall here Scheler's third philosophical truth, that every being has both *Sosein* (it is just "so", has certain characteristics) and *Dasein* (literally, it "is there", it exists). This distinction constitutes one of the foundations of his metaphysics, as we shall see. Here we must note his claim that we cannot participate in the *Dasein* of an object; existence cannot therefore be known, but only given in the form of resistance to striving. Existence is thus given to us as acting, or "conative", beings. If we were pure contemplative spirits we would not be aware of it at all. At the most primitive level of consciousness (that of what Aristotle called the vegetable soul) we have a general sense, which does not even amount to a qualifiable feeling or sensation, of something "being there" which we have to take account of. Experience of existence is thus a kind of "suffering", in which the heart's limitless desires are perforce confined.

But we can "participate in" the *Sosein* of an object. In knowledge, the object's *Sosein*, or aspects of it, actually becomes "immanent in" the mind of the knowing subject "in person", so that the knower has direct intellectual contact with it. Thus it does not require the mediation of a concept or image (let alone a "belief"). Most of Scheler's opponents argued that those suffering from illusions were undoubtedly aware of *something*. Since this could not be the real object, it must be an inadequate concept or image of it. They were then able to argue that, since illusion usually feels like knowledge to the subject, there must also be some "representative" of what is known in the mind of the one who really knows. Scheler replied that the process of *dis*illusion showed their reasoning to be false, since here we pass not from inadequate to adequate image, but from image to reality (*Sosein*). Ideas, then, are mere substitutes for what can be directly grasped.

Nor does an object have to be objectifiable to be known, as we have seen in the case of spiritual acts, so when we talk about the "object" of knowledge in its most general sense the word is also being used to encompass things that cannot actually be held before the mind's eye. The "ontological" nature of the cognitive relationship accounts for the fact that one can know something without knowing that one knows. This purely "ecstatic", non-reflexive, knowing is another indication of Man's nature as *ens amans*, as the being who naturally strives to go out of himself and share in the nature of other beings.

This basic cognitive or intuitive relationship is that of *Wissen*. Once the mind is also thinking about the object of its knowledge, *Wissen* can become *Erkennen*, where there is "a unity of coverage" between what is known and what is "meant", or where what is cognitively given "fulfils" what is intellectually intended. *Erkennen* is thus "the knowing possession of x as x". Scheler does not say a great deal about the criteria of knowledge thrown up by the institutionalisation of knowledge, but he gives us a sketch of a "foundational" series, in which, he says, the later items only make sense if the meanings of the earlier are presupposed (GW X 413). The series runs as follows: self-givenness (*something* at least must be given in the first place), adequacy or fullness of intuitive grasp (with the limiting case of total self-givenness), degree of relativity in the existence of the object (the more relative the object, the less "fullness" is possible), simple truth (the above-mentioned "coverage" is self-given), material truth and falsity, correctness and incorrectness of procedure in judging. The exact significance of the last three items, and hence the exact nature of the dependencies, is not wholly clear. We are not surprised to read that all these matters were to have been dealt with in a later work. But it will at least now be clear why Scheler denies that knowledge presupposes truth and, *a fortiori*, judgment. "There is no knowledge (*Erkenntnis*) which does not presuppose cognition (*Kenntnis*); no cognition which does not presuppose the actual presence and self-givenness of things" (GW X 397). This analysis of knowledge commended itself to Scheler not least because it seemed to possess the strengths and evade the weaknesses of both Idealism and Critical Realism, the dominant approaches of his day.

The ideas of varying cognitive adequacy or fullness, and that of the relativity of the objects of cognition are important in Scheler's analyses of three fundamental cognitive attitudes (GW X 431ff). The natural attitude gives access to the facts of ordinary practical life, accessible both through "natural perception" and also "common sense", objectified in ordinary language. These facts constitute the human "milieu", where the sun rises and sets, and where rainbows and spectral colour-qualities exist. Its objects are aspects of things in themselves relative to the needs of the animal species *Homo Sapiens*. Thus, whatever we "naturally" perceive has a double symbolic function. Firstly, it symbolises something in itself, and secondly it represents some possible use, pleasure, danger and so on. We see the red colour of the cherry both as a sign of the complete object and of what it means to us. The senses are not cognitive organs but filters which select from all possible physical objects those that are vitally important for us (an exactly parallel process occurs in internal perception). The actual knowing is, as always, a matter of "pure intuition" in perception, representation or recall. Thus the everyday world, which cuts across "inner", "outer", social and absolute spheres, is relative to the life of our species.

This relativism means that there can be no complete self-givenness of objects in the natural attitude. We can explain this by first extending the notion of object-relativity a stage further. Scheler held that our "natural attitudes" were coloured by our "racial" identity. We see the everyday world not only as "members of the human species" but also as, say, English or Japanese, at a particular point in history. Thus the ancient Greeks had a knowledge of Zeus which we cannot have. A particular Athenian of 500 B.C. might have a more or less adequate knowledge of Zeus, depending on his individual experience and powers. Scheler seems to mean that "Zeus", "Athene", "Poseidon", and so on, were symbols for objects and qualities of the absolute sphere experienced in certain culture-dependant ways. They had something in common with the objects of the religious experiences of human kind as such, but were also culturally distorted in ways which we cannot fully share. Scheler held that this relativity is extended further, as experience is also coloured by sex and by sheer individuality. Thus a genuinely hallucinated object, such as Macbeth's dagger, was an object relative to Macbeth alone. As such, Macbeth could know it more or less adequately, and be more or less faithful to his experience in talking about it.

The relativity-series "Humanity, Race, Sex, Individual" must be extended in the opposite direction if we are to understand science. Scheler claimed that the objects of the scientific attitude, which enabled us to investigate the law-like "causal" connections between material phenomena, were relative to living beings as such. Their vital-relativity came from the fact that one had to start from the world as filtered through the vital functions of human perception. But, whereas everyday knowledge still has a considerable fullness about it, and the cherry's colour is still grasped as colour, even though it is a symbol for the cherry itself, scientific knowledge is completely symbolic, and the cherry's colour disappears altogether, its place being taken by readings on a dial. Thus the "constructed" and symbolic objects of science completely lack "fullness", and are removed from the vital milieu of any particular species. It seems to follow that they might also be accessible to members of other living species starting from different vital milieus, provided that they too carried out analogous "reductions". For the point of science is to grasp the world as a field of possible movement and control, an achievement in which all living things have an interest, and which, in human beings, is prompted by the vital drive for power. Science was thus the one place where Pragmatism really applied.

Scheler's theory of science is not in the least dismissive. He insists that the scientific reduction has a legitimate "ontic" foundation — a foundation in reality. The achievements of science, which he calls *Leistungswissen* (knowledge for achievement), are beyond dispute. But he denies its supreme importance as a vehicle for really understanding the world. For one thing, its results are never more than probable and provisional. But the real point is that, if "the world" is the correlative object of all possible cognitive acts, the world of science is merely a partial *selection* from certain of its contents, the correlate of possible practical control. If fullness or adequacy of self-givenness, together with non-relativity, are required for understanding the world, then science can contribute even less than everyday knowledge. But for real fullness and absoluteness Scheler thought we must turn to philosophy.

In his "middle" period (c.1912-22) Scheler seems to have thought that the "phenomenological attitude" was a sufficient basis for philosophy. If all knowledge was based on love for (or interest in) the world, then phenomenology was distinguished by the com-plete vital disinterestedness of this love. Husserl, the first system-atic phenomenologist, had spoken of the need for putting existence (*Dasein*) "in brackets" if the essential *Sosein* of individual phenomena were to be investigated. But he understood this as a purely intellectual procedure. Scheler's conative theory of how *Dasein* is given meant that more was required. In order to penetrate the veil cast over the world by our practical or scientific interests and know it as it really is in itself, we, as spiritual persons, had actually to detach ourselves from our vital egos, thus temporarily isolating ourselves from the operation of the existence-revealing principle within us.

In his essay on the essence of philosophy (GW V), Scheler characterised philosophy as a spiritual "soaring" (*Aufschwung*), in which the entire person sought to be united with the essences of things in their essential relations. Apart from a spiritual love for "absolute value and being", one also needed humility, self-mastery and self-knowledge. Humility was necessary because one had to humble oneself as a vital, self-assertive, being in order to let the essential nature of things reveal itself.   Self-mastery and self-knowledge made possible a fullness and adequacy of philosophical intuition which all kinds of self-centred desires tended to keep within bounds. Self-mastery was also necessary to some degree for the lesser "reduction" of science.

Essences, the objects of philosophical knowledge, were in themselves always absolute objects (though they could be known more or less fully). As such they were also *a priori*. "Everything ... which 'is there' 'in itself' in lived experience and intuition, is also given *a priori* as pure whatness or essence for all possible observation or induction from what is observed" (GW X 383). Scheler called phenomenology the "desymbolisation of the world", because through it one reached the "pure" or "phenomenological" fact, in which essential connections were grounded. The latter included both logical connections, if they concerned objects as such (as in the law of contradiction), and also more specific connections confined to particular domains of objects, such as the necessary relations between colour and extension. All spheres of being had their own *a priori*.

In his earlier or middle period writings Scheler seems to assume a static and unchanging realm of essences, though in his later period he argued that they were continually evolving. But he always held, against Kant, that the domain of "*a priori* propositions" (those which are "fulfilled" in what is self-given), or the "*a priori* structure of reason", was a human product and thus not static or everywhere the same. Once essences and essential connections have been more or less adequately grasped, one's insights are put to use, and "functionalised" as selection principles for grasping further instances or forms of argument, in accordance with human purposes. Ordinary language and scientific symbol systems are more or less fixed social products of functionalisation. Thus the facts of the natural and scientific attitudes are "founded" in pure facts. But the place of human purposes in this process accounts for some of the striking differences there are between natural languages and world-views, which are the social deposits of different "functionalising" perspectives, as intellectual grasp has been more or less adequate among the leading creators of the language, or differentially biased by slightly differing practical concerns. It means also that a linguistic community's stock of *a priori* principles can develop, as functionalisation is based on more and more adequate insights. Scheler argues that the ideal of truly adequate knowledge of the *a priori* must be conceived as the task of mankind, in which all cultural communities of the past and present have their contribution to make. All this is also true of the emotional and volitional *a priori* briefly discussed in the chapter on Scheler's ethics. "The object of love becomes a form of loving;...the object of the will a form of willing". [GW V 198]

One of the greatest problems contemporary readers have with Scheler's philosophy is its lack of systematic argument, its apparently dogmatic nature. They cast around for his "criteria", and usually fail to find them. It should now be apparent that Scheler thinks of philosophy as going back behind all criteria, indeed behind all rules, formulations, concepts and other symbols, to the original cognitive and emotional experiences which form the indispen-sable basis for these things. In so far as the philosopher tries to communicate his findings, or suggest that his findings are more adequate than someone else's, he can only try "to *bring* the reader to see what, by its essence, can only be 'seen'" (GW X 391). The arguments used by philosophers are "pointers", suggestions about where to look or how to see. "He who is always inclined to ask for a criterion first of all", says Scheler, "is one who stands outside, who has no *direct* contact" with the reality he is investigating (X 381). In *Formalism* he suggests that the philosophy of criteria is the philosophy of impersonal "association" ruled by mistrust. But real philosophy, like any pursuit based on disinterested love, presupposes spiritual community, *Liebesgemeinschaft*, where personal values reign.

Although Scheler often approaches epistemological questions via his three fundamental "attitudes" (natural, scientific and phenomenological), and also talks correlatively about "the three kinds of fact", he also refers with increasing frequency to three "forms" of knowledge. These are *Leistungswissen*, knowledge for practical achievement or control, *Heilswissen*, knowledge for salvation, and *Bildungswissen*, knowledge for personal formation. The three forms are developments from the natural attitude at the respective prompting of the drive for power, the desire for salvation, and wonder.

The idea of *Leistungswissen* is the easiest to grasp, and we have already made the essential points above in discussing the natural and scientific attitudes.

Bildungswissen is sometimes called "cultural knowledge", but the basic idea seems to be that the person, in Scheler's technical sense of the word, receives individual definition through the pure values and essences which "inform" him. The word *Bildung* (its root meaning is "formation") is, of course, a traditional German term for a liberal education, especially in the humanities and arts. Through it a person receives a structure of preferred values and functionalised essences for his dealings with the world. We may add here that Scheler regarded most university philosophy, which stressed the history of philosophy, or trained its students in philosophical argument, or took a positivist attitude to science and other established disciplines, as mere *Fachwissenschaft* (systematic and specialist subject-knowledge), and quite unfitted for the task of personal formation. He saw the spread of the phenomenological attitude, with its purely receptive, yet radical, search for foundations, and essential moral preconditions, as an indispensable stage in the renewal of Western civilisation.

Unfortunately Scheler never says very much about *Heilswissen*. It seems at first to mean religious knowledge, acquired through the religious act, but it is not clear why this should make it a fundamentally separate type of knowledge. Knowledge of persons is based on particular acts without being a separate kind. He also uses the word *Heil*, salvation, in connection with the individual's task of realising his personal "essence". In *Formalism* this task is conceived in terms of achieving some kind of union with the Absolute, as the source of all essences. *Heilswissen* would thus be practical ethical-religious knowledge relative to each individual which he could only acquire in the course of actually living the moral and religious life. In his later work *Heilswissen* becomes closely bound up with metaphysics, and the individual's task is conceived as having more than personal significance, as we shall explain below. If *Leistungswissen* is for changing physical existence and *Bildungswissen* persons, *Heilswissen* is now for changing the Absolute, in solidarity with all persons and the world.

7.   METAPHYSICS AND PHILOSOPHICAL ANTHROPOLOGY

Scheler never finished his *magna opera* on metaphysics and philosophical anthropology. Until recently most students had to rely on short preparatory sketches and papers, especially "The Place of Man in the Cosmos", the pieces published as *Philosophical World-view* (all in GW X), parts of "Knowledge and Work" (GW VIII), and the second edition of *Sympathy*. But completed sections and fragments destined for both the Metaphysics and the Philosophical Anthropology have now appeared in the second and third volumes of published *Nachlass* material (GW XI and XII), and these do bring some additional enlightenment. We may say, by way of introduction, that Scheler attached enormous practical importance to metaphysics. Not only did it now include *Heilswissen*, incorporating and transcending the partial truths of Theistic religion. It also had a truly cosmic significance. It was not therefore a kind of intellectual luxury. Everyone had to have *some* idea of and attitude towards ultimate reality, so the only appropriate task was to try and help every individual attain his own metaphysical truth as adequately as possible.

How, then, was this to be done? We may begin with the short essay "Philosophical World-view", published, a few days before Scheler's death, in a Munich newspaper. Scheler here makes it clear that knowledge of values, essences and their essential relations is not enough for metaphysics, since this must also embrace the sphere of real existence. *A priori* knowledge must first be combined with the findings of the "positive" disciplines, among which Scheler includes mathematics, history and jurisprudence, as well as what we would call science, and then both these kinds of knowledge have to be combined with the findings of the "value-disciplines" ("general theory of value, aesthetics, ethics, philosophy of culture"). This combination enables us to engage in "the metaphysics of the 'boundary problems' of the positive disciplines, first order metaphysics (what is 'life' or 'matter'?), and then we can pass through it to the metaphysics of the Absolute, second order metaphysics" (GW IX 81). The final step in this "metaphysics from below upwards" would not only enable us to come into a right relationship with the Absolute, but relate the positive disciplines both to each other and also to It. Metaphysics is therefore *"Weltweisheit"* (world-wisdom) (GW XI 12). We should note here that Scheler has various alternative titles for the Absolute Being. We shall generally refer to It by the term *Ens a Se*, that is, the being that derives its being from itself.

However, between first order metaphysics, the "meta-sciences", and second order metaphysics, or *Heilswissen*, we have to engage in philosophical anthropology, since Man's "microcosmic" nature is the key to that of the *Ens a Se*. Scheler, here as so often echoing Kant, brings into play his own "transcendental argument" (GW IX 82). He assumes that the "Being of the world itself cannot depend on the contingent existence of finite Man and his empirical consciousness", and must have preceded him, and yet he also holds fast to the basic phenomenological principle that "there are *essential connections* between particular classes of spiritual acts [he also applies this to vital operations] and particular regions of *Being*". From these two premises Scheler concludes that all those "acts and operations" through which the various regions of being are given to *us* must also be ascribed to the *Ens a Se* Itself. For example, he argues (elsewhere) that Space is not absolute; its being depends on the vital impulse to move, since spatiality is the possibility of movement and given to us *in* such impulses. Combined with the assumption that "a spatially ordered world" preceded Man's appearance in it, he concludes that space must also be "posited" by a dynamic (impulsive) attribute, *Drang*, in the *Ens a Se*. This argument for the existence of an absolute or "divine" *Drang* (I shall consider the meaning of this term below) is repeated in a consideration of the existence of the material world itself, which is given to us through resistance to striving. In the same way, from the fact that essences and values both present themselves to us as having independent being of some kind, the *Ens a se* must also possess the attribute of spirit, through which It respectively thinks and loves them, since essences and values are the correlates of these spiritual acts.

Scheler says that because metaphysics incorporates findings of the "positive" disciplines it cannot yield certainty. This must also be true of philosophical anthropology, but, as he rarely makes it clear when he is appealing to necessary truth and when to empirical findings, it is not easy to know exactly what he thought was merely probable, and what certain. But metaphysics was too important to be neglected just because of the probabilistic element. This is because its ultimate point was salvation (*Heil*), involving complete participation in the Absolute. We saw above that philosophy as *Bildungswissen* involved the total engagement of the spiritual person in the ideal realm of values and essences. This necessarily involved more than reason; it also included feeling and love. But as *Heilswissen*, in the late works, it also involves the non-spiritual impulsive or vital side of the human being, since the Absolute includes real existence, which cannot be in any sense directly given to spirit. Thus the way to metaphysical participation in ultimate reality is twofold. It is spiritual, but also "Dionysiac" (or vital). And because the world (even in its essential structure) is not something given once and for all, but is in *process*, being always the correlative of some act, and thus continually brought forth by the interplay of the divine spirit and the divine *Drang*, second order metaphysics can be characterised as "*Nachproduktion der Welt aus ihrem gotthaften Grund*" (GW XI 91), — as a kind of recapitulation of and identification with continuous creation through one's whole spiritual and vital being. The metaphysics of the Absolute, then, cannot be mere *study*; it requires *Einsatz*, vital involvement and affirmation. We have said something about the "ascesis" necessary for spiritual acts above. On the vital side, *Einsatz* involves letting oneself become one in feeling and impulse with the vital force underlying reality by putting our spiritual centre and our sense of individual embodiedness out of action. This is, of course, the

Einsfühlung, or "cosmo-vital identification", we have already come across in our survey of the first part of *Sympathy*.

The two most fundamental features of Scheler's metaphysics are the "dualism" of Spirit and *Drang* and the separation of *Sosein* from *Dasein*. In the philosophy of the middle period God is interpreted as pure Spirit, and the real world of material forces, physical objects and living things is regarded as His creation *ex nihilo*. But Scheler was always much occupied with the problem of evil. In *On the Eternal* he says that the doctrine of the Fall, including that of a super-human spirit (an angel), is a "truth of reason" for any Theistic world-view. But reflection on the first world war, and other catastrophic events of the time, had gradually convinced him that there was too much evil in the world for it to have been the creation of God as *Summum Bonum* and omnipotent Spirit, even granted the freedom of created spirits to choose it. His solution, reinforced by various empirical claims about the precarious and short-lived nature of spiritual and high cultural achievements, and their inevitable adulteration if they are to be widely appreciated, was the doctrine of the Spirit's original *powerlessness*, and the claim that the real existence of the world was the work of another principle within the *Ens a Se*, namely the divine *Drang*.

In "The Place of Man" Scheler uses the duality of Spirit and *Drang* to distinguish men from other animals. He argues that Man is like an animal in every essential respect except one — his possession of spirit. The early part of this work includes a penetrating analysis of what he calls the three essentially distinct levels of life, or the psychic powers that constitute the "inwardness" of all living things. First comes the undifferentiated "feeling-drive", an uncomprehending "towards" and "away from" what respectively serves or threatens vital existence, to which vegetable existence is confined. There is no "reporting back" of any kind here, and thus the feeling-drive is purely ecstatic, or outward directed. But already we find the phenomenon of (non-purposive) expression. It is at this level that reality is given to us. Then comes "instinct", especially characteristic of non-mammalian animal species, which Scheler defines as meaningful behaviour, of fixed periodicity, which serves the species as a whole, and whose success is independent of the number of times it is performed. He sums it up as a "unity of unreflective foreknowledge and action". Last come the two co-ordinate forms of trial and error learning, based on the conditioned reflex, and "practical intelligence", which he analyses as a kind of insight, enabling its possessor to master wholly new practical situations without recourse to instinctive "knowledge" or trial and error. Thanks to his acquaintance with the work of Köhler and other ethologists Scheler had a much higher opinion of the capacities of animals than many philosophers, and had no hesitation in ascribing practical intelligence to chimpanzees, for example.

Scheler shows that human beings still operate at all these levels of vital functioning. But he argues that they also possess something quite different, namely "objectivity", or "world-openness", the ability to put their vital concerns aside and see and respond to the essential *Sosein* and value of things in themselves. They can also put the interests of other people before their own, and even sacrifice their own lives. These and other manifestations of Spirit are not to be found among animals. They cannot get free of their specific *milieus*, but necessarily live their lives "ecstatically immersed" in the successive vital concerns of the moment. Even their occasional intelligent, "aesthetic" and altruistic behaviour is still governed by their various vital impulses. Spirit, then, is an attribute of Man and of the *Ens a Se*. Since it is itself the principle which enables us to "objectify", it cannot itself be objectified, and exists solely as act.

We have already noted why Scheler, in his late work, ascribed *Drang* to the *Ens a Se*. We have to understand it as what is common to both the power of impulse or vital energy, which we feel in ourselves and sympathetically grasp in all other living things, and also what we can sense and observe acting on our and other bodies as the "material" forces of nature. The ultimate unity of these forces is given in *Einsfühlung*, cosmo-vital identification with "creation", where the whole world appears as one organism. *Drang* is, then, the force that underlies all real existence.

But the world we perceive is not primarily a field of "concentrations of force" but of material things. Scheler, who held to the Gestalt

psychological principle of the primacy of imagination over perception, uses two important ideas to account for this, *Bilder* (singular
Bild), and *Drangphantasie*. *Bilder* are the phenomenal forms through
which real centres of force are given to us in perception. They are
relative to life as such and not to individuals. This makes them
"absolute for us" as vital beings, and licences us to talk quite properly
of errors in perception. Although they are *"transbewusst"* — outside
consciousness — they are only objective appearances, made of the
same "stuff" as dreams and fantasies. As such, again following the law
that correlates act or function and sphere of being, they must be the
work of imagination, and, since they are independent of human
imagination, they must be the work of a power of productive
imagination in the divine *Drang*. Thus, the *Bilder* of perception are
the work of *Drangphantasie*. "Nature" is the product of the imagina-
tive "play" of the Absolute, as *Drang*. Most human perception is in
fact limited by practical concerns, as in the "natural attitude". The
attempt to perceive things in their whole nature as *Bilder* is aesthetic
contemplation, for which one must perceive "ecstatically", totally
oblivious of one's self and its individual interests, and wholly
absorbed in the appearance of the object.

We need to describe two other constituents of Scheler's philosophy
of *Drang* to complete this picture — *Alleben* ('all-life') and Eros.
"All-life" is a necessary aspect of the divine *Drang* because of the
phenomenal distinction between centres of pure physical force and
centres of vital force (living things). Scheler held the primal field of
force to be in itself "anarchic". The formal mechanical laws of physics
were themselves *Bilder*, and had only statistical validity. But pure
physical energy was only one manifestation of the divine *Drang*.
Equally original was *Drang* as life-energy, or *Alleben*. This principle
of all life had to be thought of as harnessing physical forces to advance
itself by the incorporation of available "constellations" of energy into
living forms produced by *Drangphantasie*. The principle by which it
did this was that of Eros, which always aims at the noblest or most
perfect forms available at the time, the highest vital values producible
within a given "budget" of energy, consistent also with a maximum

of production for the least expenditure of energy (the principle of practical intelligence). At the human level Eros is the vital component of the artist's activity, and results from the diversion or sublimation of sexual drive-energy into the functions of seeing, hearing, and so on, so that aesthetic contemplation becomes both possible and enjoyable.

We have now, therefore, seen something of Spirit and *Drang*. Scheler describes them, in the manner of Spinoza, as two among the infinite attributes of the eternally unchanging "Substance", or *Ens a se*. They are jointly responsible for all creation, and, in their variously meted "partial functions", they are also constitutive of human beings. We must now pass to consider the relation between them.

This has often been represented by expositors as a kind of conflict, even as an externalisation by Scheler of his own moral struggle. But *Nachlass* volumes XI and XII of the collected works give a different picture. For example, Scheler says that *Geist* and *Drang* are not enemies in reality, though this might be said by "the over-sublimated ascetic and the impulsive man of guilty conscience" (GW XII 113). He also says that *Drang* "eternally strives for the Idea" — for the essence which will give perfect form to its otherwise spiritually "blind" productions — and that Spirit "eternally awaits ... the effective initiative of *Drang*", so that its ideal forms and values may be translated into reality. We also read that Eros, striving perpetually for what is higher and more beautifully formed within the limitations of its own vital (i.e. spiritually blind) sphere and its vital "maximis- ing" tendency, is itself a kind of precursor of *Geist* in the sphere of life, and steers vitality in the direction of spirit (GW XII 234). The fact is that, in Scheler's total conception, *Geist* and *Drang* need each other, and are, to a considerable extent, each already searching for what the other can offer.

The impression of a conflict between the two partly arises from the way Scheler describes their interaction in "The Place of Man". The spiritual act is here called "ascetic". It is made possible by Man's saying "no" to life. In order that vital energy should be put into the Spirit's service, spiritual ideas and values have to be "held out" like "bait" before the "lurking" impulses. But this hunting or hijacking imagery is not an essential part of the picture. He often uses the more neutral picture of *Leiten* and *Lenken*. The person directs (*leitet*) drive-energy by means of spiritual values, or inhibits or "de-inhibits" (*lenkt*) the physical movements which are the executive developments of vital motivation. This hydraulic imagery shows Scheler's interest in the Freudian idea of sublimation, which he describes as the freeing of drive-energy from the drives themselves, and which is already at work in Eros. It is part of this theory that human beings have more drive-energy than they need to meet the demands of the sexual-reproductive and nurturing drive, a surplus confined to this drive because it alone, unlike the power-drive and the "economic" drive, was essentially other-directed (GW XII 231). Eros itself, which leads vital life to the very threshold of Spirit, is "biologically necessary", and provides a defence against "the [biological] dangers of over-population, stereotyping and the anarchy of drive-impulses confined by instinct" (GW XII 234). In general, then, life itself looks in the direction of spirit to solve its own problems, and the "no" which Spirit addresses to life relates to a vitality left, almost *per impossibile*, to its own devices. Spirit and *Drang* are, after all, both attributes of the same absolute being, and, in Man, of the same living beings. Scheler does often speak in terms of a "tension" between them, since each sets its own kind of limits to the unfolding of the other. But the essential point is that they represent different orders of being, and cannot therefore be in opposition like rival principles of the same order.

A related matter is the principle of Spirit's "powerlessness". We must first stress that this does not entail the powerlessness of the *Ens a Se*. As *Drang*, the *Ens a Se is* power. Nor does it mean that the Spirit, either in Man or in the Godhead, cannot in any sense "do" anything. What Spirit cannot do is directly alter the balance of power in the sphere of (physical and psychic) reality. Its powerlessness is therefore a lack of quantifiable or "gradable" power (GW XII 160), and its activity "lacks intensity" (GW XII 267). The "spiritual power" — as we might put it — which is needed for self-collection, or to inhibit and de-inhibit drive-energy, is not of the material order. Once more, the basic principle is the difference between two different orders of being.

Whether Scheler really makes their interaction intelligible in this way is a difficult matter to decide. But it seems true of experience that the term "will-power" does denote a kind of effectiveness which eludes objective grasp and analysis. Scheler is also surely right in his claim that the will cannot simply "dictate" what the person will do. There must already be, not just a "reason", but an available impulse, if an idea or value is to be realised. Hence the attempts of a long line of reductively inclined thinkers to explain it away.

It is time now to look in more detail at Scheler's conception of "world-history". Before the start of the world-process, but outside time, there is the *Ens a Se*, or the "eternal substance", eternally "positing" (*setzend*) itself (GW XI 212). This positing consists in self-love, self-contemplation and self-willing as *Geist*, albeit in the mode of potentiality, and, likewise potentially, in a striving or "thirst" for real existence as *Drang*. This potential activity of two of Its attributes means that even the *Ens a Se* can be said to be in a state of unknowable becoming, or process. The potentiality also indicates that this originary self-positing involves inhibition, and is another element in the "tension" in the *Ens a Se*.

The world-process achieves reality when the *Ens a Se*, as Spirit, wills to de-inhibit its self-positing, thus transforming it into the mode of actuality. The motive-power for this comes from Eros, the vital mode of the divine self-love. The beginning of the world's history is described as a relaxing of the tension, but also as a permitting. In a passage very reminiscent of Christian apologetics Scheler pictures "God as spirit" as weeping bitterly for all the evil and suffering which this release *might* bring about. As Spirit God determines the structure of the possible world, and thus knows in advance what evils may come, but has no knowledge of what they will actually be. Hence the admission of the world-process involves risk. "Yet God as Spirit 'believes' ... in the victory of His idea, the idea of His self-love", in which "all things will be perfected in Him", and that evil will not triumph. Hence it is a venture of love (GW XI 206f).

The world-process is thus the self-realisation of God, as the Spirit acquires real existence in the form of "body". At first, it seems, the world-process lacks the full presence of Spirit, since Man is the only place where Spirit appears in full self-consciousness. But the divine Spirit sets a priori limits to the original productive interplay between *Alleben* and the purely physical concentrations of force also produced by *Drang*. We have here, in fact, both the *Leiten* and *Lenken* already described as the way in which the Spirit influences reality in general, and an analogous process between Eros-guided *Alleben* and purely dynamic reality. The purpose of this is the concentration of all physical energy into the bodies of individual living things, the more perfect the better. The meaning of life in itself is indeed the enrichment of *Alleben*, which "learns" from its ventures as individuals and species sink back at death once more into the stream of life. Scheler therefore denies that species evolve naturally from one another. Rather, they are produced anew under the guidance of Eros out of the material of *Drangphantasie* (within the prevailing physical restraints). As for Man, the microcosm, who unites in himself all regions of being and, through his non-specialisation, exhibits in developed form all that *Alleben* has "learnt" through its countless specific "embodiments", he was bound to appear at some time.

The "process" assumptions of Scheler's metaphysics mean that this necessary tendency towards the emergence of Man cannot be accounted for by the actual *pre-existence* of the Idea of Man. For ideas are neither pre-given nor given "in" their instantiations, as Plato and Aristotle respectively held, but given "with" them, as new things come into existence. Thus Scheler continues to insist on the distinction between *Dasein* and *Sosein* by involving both *Drang* and Spirit as equal partners in the continual production of the world. He again uses the analogy of art to make this clearer. The artist does not start out with a blue-print of what he is going to create, but, at most, with a rough and highly provisional conception. The "*Urbild*", or "*a priori* appearance", presented in the work emerges in the artist's interaction with the physical "material" which presents it. Neither the physical medium nor the *Urbild* takes priority.

Scheler also characterises the emergence of Man as "the Godhead's struggle to reach up to Itself, to Its own reality in miniature". The full significance of the emergence of Man is, then, that the Godhead (*Gottheit*), that is, the still imperfect, because still "becoming", attribute of Spirit, most fully realises Itself in him. Thus, in this late philosophy, any spiritual act is at once the productive work of the Godhead in Man, and of Man in, or "after", the Godhead. Analogous things must be said of vital functioning, the "demonic" side of the world-process. The "*Urbild*" presented in a great work of art is a real addition to the perceivable world, not a copy of something already there. It is as though the creative artist actually returns to the timeless realm of world-becoming, where the Absolute Spirit has not yet made choice of what ideas and essences shall come into existence, and makes himself co-agent in the emergence of new or purer *Urbilder*, and thus makes possible actual perceptions of types or of an adequacy hitherto unavailable (GW XI 35). In the same way the philosopher's grasp of essence is not a purely intellectual insight into something always "there", but a "*Nacherzeugen*", a recapitulatory production in identification with the Absolute Spirit (GW XI 91).

The real difference in the world-process marked by the appearance of Man seems to be that now the Absolute Spirit knows itself, and the goal of world-history can be deliberately approached, rather than being wholly dependant on the still vitally-inspired generation of Eros, which only *tends* somewhat haphazardly towards spirit. This goal is the complete realisation or empowering of Spirit and spiritualisation of *Drang*, the total "interpenetration" of the two principles, which will fully resolve the tension in the *Ens a Se*, and mark the transition from Godhead to God. There will be "perpetual peace", not only in the world, which is now become "God's body" (though not the body of the *Ens a Se*), but also in Man and God. The "solidarity" between God, Man and World is much emphasised by Scheler. Man, with his ability to make free choices, even life-denying ones, and thus accelerate the process of interpenetration, becomes the key to the world-process. But Scheler also says that there is nothing cosmically fundamental about empirical human nature, and the actual world we know. For worlds can die, life's manifestations can be absorbed again into *Alleben*, and there will be new and better "worlds", as Spirit and *Drang* both "learn" (GW XI 198).

The idea of "interpenetration" at the level of human history is explained in such terms as these: "Ideas and moral values very gradually acquire a certain `power' in that they become increasingly bound up with interests and enthusiasms and all the institutions based on them" (GW IX 81). Conversely, even the most powerful mass movements depend on the spiritual will of "great leaders". At the individual level interpenetration has taken place when spiritual activity acquires the force of habit, or the power of conscience, and vitally significant behaviour (eating, sex) regularly becomes an occasion for the celebration of spiritual value. Scheler also says that over-intellectualised and politically over-moralised Western Man needs to "de-sublimate" on occasion, and allow the forces of life to "take over" for a while. There is always an appropriate balance between the Apollonian and the Dionysiac laid down in the individual value-essence of every person or *Gesamtperson*, to which we can either say "no" or not say "no". The main point of "interpenetration", which is variously exemplified in "Man in the World-Age of Adjustment" (GW IX), is that every action and process should exhibit a maximum of spiritual value and perfect essence combined with real effectiveness.

We may end this survey with a few remarks about Scheler's treatment of human history as presented in his "Sociology of Knowledge" (GW VIII). He here argues against both Materialist theories of history, such as those of Marx and Gobineau, and Spiritualist ones, such as those of Hegel and many Christian thinkers. The analysis takes for granted the original powerlessness of Spirit and the bounds of essential possibility which sets limits to real developments. He distinguishes "real" (i.e. *Drang*) factors and spiritual factors, in a way which will now need no illustration, and argues that each sort of historical factor has a limiting effect on the other. Thus spiritual factors can, through personal agency, influence the development of real factors by *temporarily* displacing them, whereas real factors can influence spiritual development in that only a certain range of spiritual achievements is realisable for any given constellation of them. There are three kinds of real factors, corresponding to the thrée major drive-forms taken by the divine *Drang* in the human vital constitution: economic factors, racial and kinship factors (developments of the nutritive drive) and power factors. The course of real events is determined according to fixed laws by the particular combinations of these three factors which obtain in the leading representatives of the groups and cultures concerned. Societies grow up and age just like individuals, and at each period of a group's life one of these factors will outweigh the others. Thus a Marxist analysis will only apply to ageing societies, when the economic drive is predominant, and its preeminence will merely *limit* the forms of familial-kinship and political institutions. These rather abstract analyses are followed by some highly interesting discussions of religion, metaphysics and science, both as forms of knowledge and as social institutions, and their relation to various real factors in history. The best of these discussions go far to illuminate the inner "logic" of science, technology, religion and metaphysics, and to relate them convincingly, through necessary tendencies, to types of social climate, political organisation, economic conditions, kinship structures, and other real factors. There is much here on the striking differences between the prevailing cultures of India, China and the West.

It has to be said that, even with the extensive fragments and sketches published in GW XI and XII, Scheler's metaphysics is difficult to interpret. One may perhaps follow Heidegger and Hartmann and stress his courageous determination to be consistent to the bitter end, or his Catholic critics who see here not only a lack of fidelity to the fundamental insights of his earlier thought, but an almost wilful adoption of positions he had himself previously pilloried. Scheler affirms that Man has far more than a fundamentally receptive role to play in the world, since he is an active partner in its production, yet he now seems to deny the individual's ultimate metaphysical uniqueness, by calling him a unique "concentration of the divine spirit", and a mere wave, or functional centre, in the sea of *Alleben*. The metaphysics does breathe the spirit of religious and moral seriousness (it has been said that Scheler goes wrong theologically in that he conflates creation and redemption), yet the distinctions and felt relations between God, Man and World which seem the usual source of this seriousness seem so blurred that the reader may feel thoroughly confused. Nevertheless one cannot for long escape the impression of a profound and fascinating thinker grappling with the roots of being to make sense of the Whole, and always trying to keep his speculation in touch with his own experience of life, and the findings of those working at the frontiers of knowledge. Noone interested in philosophical anthropology can afford to ignore him. As regards metaphysics, he at the very least reopens the great questions once more, and, by linking them to questions about human nature and the meaning of life, shows how they may be, and indeed ought to be, engaged in by every one capable of understanding them.

8.   WHY READ SCHELER TODAY?

In chapter 6 ("Forms of Knowledge"), I briefly referred to the distinction which Scheler draws between philosophy as *Fachwissenschaft* and as material for *Bildung*. According to this the *Fach*-philosopher tends to be a narrow specialist, who will be interested in what can be clearly defined or solved in accordance with agreed procedures. He will see philosophy as one subject of study among others. The *Bildungs*-philosopher will, on the other hand, take a wide view of "all time and all existence", and be ready to sacrifice clarity and demonstrability to profundity and comprehensiveness. He will see philosophy as comprising all "subjects". It is tempting to say that the neglect of Scheler which prevails in many university departments of philosophy today is largely the result of the *Fach* conception of philosophy prevailing there, and that he is really a *Bildungs*-philosopher, one who will transform one's outlook, and hence one's life.

This suggestion contains some oversimplification (perhaps the perfect philosopher will have a foot in both camps), but I think it also contains more than a grain of truth. Only one who had already decided how the fundamental questions of philosophy should be approached (or assigned them magisterially to the world of non-questions) could doubt that Scheler was a genuine philosopher. He lived and breathed philosophy (according to his third wife he would begin verbally philosophising when dressing in the morning). It seems, then, extremely likely that Scheler is neglected by many philosophers because they do not share his conception of philosophy. They would no doubt reply that Scheler's faults are such that he could not satisfy any reasonable conception of philosophy. To which the answer is that all philosophers have their faults, and Scheler's are certainly both many and glaring. The question is: do his virtues atone for his failures? And clearly the answer one gives to this question will depend on one's conception of philosophy.

Let us, then, return to Scheler's *Bildung* conception of philosophy. If his philosophy *is* worth reading, then it will, more or less clearly, "speak" to us if we are prepared to listen. We will here be responding in love to the exemplary value of Scheler the intellectual *Vorbild* (as Scheler tells us he responded to Spinoza), through which we shall gain not necessarily a number of "truths" or cogent arguments, but a more adequate and comprehensive vision of things, a growing appreciation of neglected distinctions and relations, a deeper feeling for values and disvalues, at the prompting of our own value-essences.

One of the stumbling-blocks lying in the way of the modern analytic philosopher is the metaphorical, even poetic, language which Scheler often uses. Parts of the metaphysics even remind one of Plato's myths. But the test here is the same. If we can read him in a genuinely non-combative and searching spirit, actually wanting him to make sense, so that his words awaken echoes in our experience, then they are doing their job, which is to help us to see what (Scheler insists) can only be *seen*. Many modern philosophers, yearning for the precision of science, will find this solution to the problem of philosophical meaning inadequate, and will demand public criteria. The burden of Scheler's philosophy is that criteria are always second-best, and that arguments are person-relative aids to intuition. It is noteworthy that, although modern analytic philosophers have exalted argument at the expense of insight in their search for agreement, they are as far as ever from agreement in anything of fundamental importance. To engage with Scheler is, then, to have one's basic philosophical presuppositions challenged and perhaps altered.

What else could today's philosophers learn from Scheler? Obviously the place he gives to love, feeling and emotion in the whole intellectual and practical life of Man is extremely suggestive and important. There are signs today that thinkers may be growing more receptive to such ideas. Then there is his claim that ethics must ultimately be founded on the feeling-apprehension of value. The usual rejection of this idea in English-speaking circles stems as much from a practical pedagogical (and increasingly political) concern as from a contemplative. Scheler's attempt to link ethics closely to philosophical psychology and our experience of the Absolute seems an important antidote to this. The possibility of pedagogy is linked in fact to the theory of *Vorbilder*. This also does much to account for the extraordinary influence of particular thinkers in our own intellectual life, and for intellectual fashion in general (or should we account for this by resort to psychic "infection"?). Scheler's personalist social philosophy helps us to see the limitations of the liberal conception of the "community of all rational beings". And yet he is never reductive in his approach to humanity, accepting both our obvious kinship with animals and our spiritual calling. Scheler's dualist picture will be ruled out of hand by many thinkers today, yet it is always being smuggled back into philosophy somehow (e.g. in the distinction between reasons and causes, or between persons and things). Then there is his abiding concern with the Absolute. His increasingly open and speculative approach to this, while never rejecting for one moment the idea of an absolute *sphere*, might at least serve to wean many Western intellectuals away from the childish ideas of God they have rejected. This question is clearly related to our idolisation of science. Scheler presents us with the example of a thinker well acquainted with and respectful of science but nevertheless refusing to allow philosophy and the human spirit to be judged in its terms.

We may finally point to certain aspects of Scheler's thought that are peculiarly relevant to the political agenda of our modern world. One cannot read far in his social philosophy without realising that he is addressing a political situation which has a lot in common with our own. He too faces a breakdown of the old order, loss of the sense of community, triumph of material values, depersonalisation, anarchy in the spheres of education, culture and thought. He was, like us, especially aware of the loss of authority in modern society. He represents an "élitist" position integrally linked to his Personalism. Selfless dedication to higher values is essential to humanity, but the only way to it is through love of the individuals and social persons who conspicuously embody them. The existence of a value hierarchy counts for nothing in the real world unless there are social hierarchies, *Vorbilder* and élites.

Scheler also presents us with the beginnings of a philosophy of the Environment. His work on sympathetic identification with all living things and on the relation between the vital and the spiritual in human life should light up an important gap in ecological thinking. At present this seems to be either still too closely linked with *Leistungswissen* (the natural world as to be only *prudently* exploited) or with the pagan vitalism he himself combatted in some of his contemporaries. There must be a right balance between spirit and life.

There is lastly Scheler's thinking about *Ausgleich* — mutual adjustment. He saw very clearly that the world was contracting; that peoples and races were inevitably coming closer together. But he also saw the enormous losses that would result if this *Ausgleich* meant a levelling of spiritual differences in the common pursuit either of hedonic and utility values or of a spurious universality of Reason. All individuals and all social persons see and feel things from slightly differing perspectives. In order that their insights may be combined one day into a comprehensive vision of reality and value their distinctness must not be destroyed.

Scheler is an immensely encouraging philosopher, despite the tragic tone he sometimes employs. To read him is a stimulating and invigorating experience, even if his faults are often exasperating. The range of his concerns, the profundity of his insights, his breadth of vision and sympathy make the study of his works a richly rewarding task.

BIBLIOGRAPHICAL NOTES

Collected Works

Of the *Gesammelte Werke* (GW) twelve volumes have so far been published. They were formerly brought out by the Francke Verlag, Berne and Munich, but are now being published by the Bouvier Verlag (Herbert Grundmann), Bonn. The following list gives volume number, date of first publication, title, (short) translation of title, notable works included (where appropriate) and the more important related English translations:

I (1971) *Frühe Schriften* (Early works). Includes theses.

II (1954) *Formalismus in der Ethik und die materiale Wertethik* (Formalism), tr. "Formalism in Ethics and Non-Formal Ethics of Values" by M.S.Frings and R.Funk, Evanston: Northwestern U.P., 1973.

III (1955) *Vom Umsturz der Werte* (On the Subversion of Values). A collection of pre-Great War papers, including "Resentment", tr. "Ressentiment" by W.Holdheim, ed. L.A.Coser, New York: Free Press, 1961. See also under *Translations* below.

IV (1982) *Politisch-pädagogische Schriften* (Political and Pedagogical writings). Includes the "War books".

V (1954) *Vom Ewigen im Menschen* (On the Eternal), tr. "On the Eternal in Man" by B.Noble, London: SCM Press, 1960.

VI (1963) *Schriften zur Soziologie und Weltanschauungslehre* (Papers on Sociology and the Theory of World-views). A varied collection of papers and essays.

VII (1973) *Wesen und Formen der Sympathie* (Sympathy), tr. "The Nature of Sympathy" by P.Heath, ed. W.Stark, London: Routledge & Kegan Paul, 1954.

VIII (1960) *Die Wissensformen und die Gesellschaft* (The Forms of Knowledge and Society). Includes "Problems of a Sociology of Knowledge", tr. under that title by M.S.Frings, ed. K.W.Stikkers, London: Routledge & Kegan Paul, 1980, and "Knowledge and Work" (important work on the value and limits of Pragmatism).

IX (1975) *Späte Schriften* (Later writings), including "The Place of Man in the Cosmos", tr. "Man's Place in Nature" by H.Meyerhoff, New York: Noonday Press, 1961, and "Philosophical World-view", tr. "Philosophical Perspectives" by O.Haac, Boston: Beacon Press, 1958. See also under *Translations* below.

X (1957) *Nachlass* material relating to ethics and phenomenology (see below for translations).

XI (1979) *Nachlass* material relating to theory of knowledge and metaphysics.

XII (1987) *Nachlass* material relating to philosophical anthropology.

XIII will contain *Nachlass* material on philosophy of history and society, and the series will be closed with a volume (XIV) of Inedita and Varia.

Bibliographies

A very thorough bibliography of works by and about Scheler was compiled by W.Hartmann and published by the Friedrich Frommann

Verlag (Günther Holzboog) as *Max Scheler: Bibliographie,* Stuttgart-Bad Cannstatt, 1963. This was continued to 1974 by M.S.Frings, whose "Bibliography 1963-1974" can be found in *Max Scheler — Centennial Essays*, ed. M.S.Frings, Martinus Nijhoff: The Hague, 1974. The latest bibliography of Scheler's own work is contained in GW XII (1987). Information about the contents of the *Nachlass* can be found in *Die Nachlässe der Münchener Phänomenologen in der Bayerischen Staatsbibliothek*, ed. E.Avé-Lallemant, Wiesbaden: Harrassowitz, 1975.

Translations

Hartmann's bibliography contains a list of translations of Scheler's works up to 1963, and this is continued, for English translations only, in Frings's bibliography. The list of English translations is taken up to 1978 by Frings and K.W.Stikkers in *Journal of the British Society for Phenomenology*, IX, 3, 1978, pp207f. In addition to the translations mentioned above, quite a number of lesser works have been put into English. The following may especially be found useful: *Selected Philosophical Essays*, tr. D.Lachterman, Evanston: Northwestern University Press, 1973. It contains "The Idols of Self-knowledge" (GW III), "Ordo Amoris", "Phenomenology and the Theory of Cognition", "The Theory of Three Facts" (all GW X) and "Idealism and Realism" (GW IX).

General Introductions

The following have been published in English:

Max Scheler: a concise introduction into the world of a great thinker, M.S.Frings, Pittsburgh, Pa.: Duquesne University Press, 1965.

Max Scheler, E.Kelly, Boston, Mass.: Twayne Publishers, 1977 (Twayne's world leaders series, no. 55).

Max Scheler: the man and his work, J.H.Nota, S.J., Chicago, Ill.:

Franciscan Herald Press, 1983.

A substantial section on Scheler, which surveys his work from the point of view of its place in the history of phenomenology, is contained in:
The Phenomenological Movement: a historical introduction, Vol.1, H.Spiegelberg, The Hague: Martinus Nijhoff, 1976.

Better and fuller than all these, and likely to be linguistically accessible to many English readers is:
La Philosophie de Max Scheler: son évolution et son unité, M.Dupuy, Paris: Presses Universitaires de France, 2 vols., 1959.

Life

No large-scale biography has yet been written. The best (though largely unsympathetic) introduction to the life available in English is:

Max Scheler 1874-1928, J.R.Staude, New York: The Free Press, 1967.

To those who read even a little German the following illustrated account can be recommended:

Max Scheler: in Selbstzeugnissen und Bilddokumenten, W.Mader, Reinbek bei Hamburg: Rowohlt Taschenbuch Verlag, 1980 (in the *Bildmonographien* series).

Index